Memory Lane
DERBY

THE ROD JEWELL COLLECTION

Memory Lane
DERBY

Evening Telegraph

Breedon Books
Publishing Company
Derby

First published in Great Britain by
The Breedon Books Publishing Company Limited
Breedon House, 44 Friar Gate, Derby, DE1 1DA.
1998

The author would be pleased to hear from anyone wishing to dispose of
postcards, photographs and collections of anywhere in the world but
especially local. Any image in this book may be purchased as a quality
sepia print. Please telephone 01773 852877

ISBN 1 85983 119 2

Printed and bound by Butler & Tanner Ltd., Selwood Printing Works, Caxton
Road, Frome, Somerset.

Colour separations by Freelance Repro, Leicester.

Jackets printed by Lawrence-Allen, Avon.

Contents

Dedication

To the little-known 'back street photographer' Charles William Lee, and Mum and Dad.

Acknowledgements

Grateful thanks to Alan and Clive Champion, the Derby-based postcard dealers, for relieving me of funds for postcards.

John Bean, Andrea Fitt, Lianne Jewell, Lila and Frank Fellows, Beryl and Roy Salt for research.

Special thanks to Linda Bentley and Julie Fellows-Jewell for their diligence in putting the manuscript on disc, and to John Archer for the collecting inspiration and much material.

Introduction

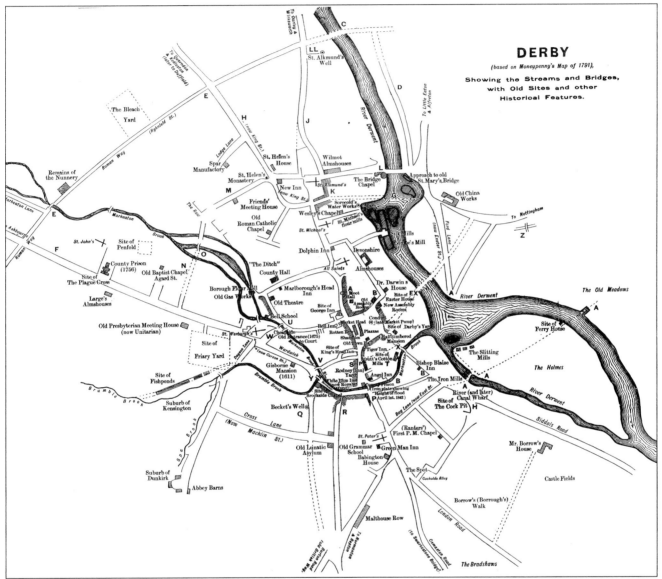

This map of Derby town and its roads and historical features was produced by Bemrose & Sons Ltd, the map engravers and printers, and was based on Moneypenny's Map of 1791.

THE roads into and out of Derby have all played their part in the town's rich and fascinating story. The following ancient poem entitled *The Mayor and the Coachman* describes a bygone trip down Derby's 'memory lane'.

The Mayor he had a Coachman and the Coachman's name was John
Said His Worship to the Coachman, "Take your wages and begone"
"I want a better Coachman for I'm going to take a drive"
Said John, "I am the finest Coachman that you can find alive"
"And if you'll let me drive to-day, I'll show I can't be beat"
"For I'll drive you all round Derby and I'll not go through a street"
Said His Worship, "John you must be mad, but still I'll humour you"

A *c.*1907 view down Camp Street, Chester Green, looking towards Marcus Street, with the corner store on Mark Street mid-right.

"But remember that you lose your place the first street you go through "
The Mayor jumped in his carriage, the Coachman on his seat
They drove down the *Duffield Road* which we all know is not a street
Lodge Lane then, and *Willow Row* the Coachman drives again
And at the top turns to the left and into *Walker Lane*
All Saints' Church, St Mary's Gate, then up *Bold Lane* he drives
And thus to keep out of a street John artfully contrives
Through *Cheapside* into *Friar Gate,* said His Worship in a pet
"Dash my wig and spectacles I think he'll do it yet"
Uttoxeter the Old Road the Coachman drives again
Down *Lonsdale Place* turns to the right and into *Stockbrook Lane*
 Woods Lane then and *Burton Road;* up *Mill Hill Lane* he'll trot
Normanton Road and *Babington Lane* then right across the *Spot*
From the *Spot* up *London Road* then the *Borough's Walk*
Siddals Road, The Morledge to the *Market* for some pork
"We are at *The Corporation,*" said the Coachman, "don't you think?"
"We'd better wet our whistles" - so His Worship stood a drink
The Coachman then continued down *Meadow Road, Exeter Place* and *Nottingham Road* and right across
    Bridge Gate
"Stop! Stop! Stop! Stop!" His Worship cried. "You must give in, you're beat
For if you drive another yard you'll have to take *King Street*"
Said John, "Oh no, that will not do – I have another move"
Darley Lane and *North Parade* and into *Darley Grove*
"*Darley Grove* to *Duffield Road,*" said the Coachman. "There's your treat. I've driven you all round Derby
    and I've not been through a street"

The date of this poem must be some time between 1861 (when the Corporation Hotel opened in the Cattle Market) and 1887 (when Stockbrook Lane became numbered as part of Stockbrook Street).

Derby's social history is also preserved by such fine photographers as John Mayle & Sons, Charles S.Swift, Charles F.Dereske, Treble Studio, Alfred Woodmansee and Hurst & Wallis who succeeded Richard Keene Ltd as the official photographers to the Derby Borough Council.

However, several of the photographs in this book were taken by amateurs who have helped tremendously in capturing Derby reflections of a bygone age.

The Primitive Methodist Chapel on Dean Street in 1906.

Maids' frocks, costumes and coats are advertised in this late 1920s interior view of Thurman & Malin, the draper's on St Peter's Street

Cups at 1s 6d and the style of pottery help date this 1950s interior view of J. & A. Flower, the china and glass merchants who had premises on Cockpit Hill, The Strand and East Street.

However, the purpose of this book is not to keep to the roads but to also take the reader around the many back streets of Derby. And to this end we must be truly grateful to Derby's 'back street photographer' Charles William Lee.

Charles William Lee was an excellent photo-

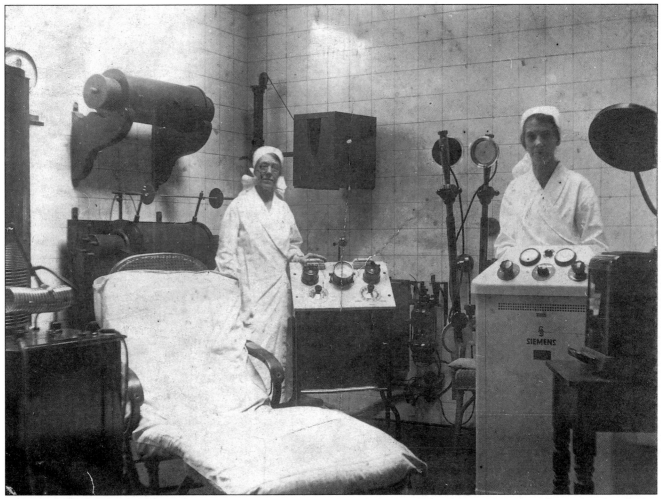

Few people like hospitals and the Siemans apparatus and other horrific looking electrical treatment equipment featured in this *c.*1920s view inside the Derbyshire Royal Infirmary would hardly change their minds.

grapher who should be ranked alongside Derby's best – Richard Keene, William Winter, Frederick Boyes and Francis William Scarratt. He operated for a short period only, from *c.*1904 to *c.*1911 when he produced approximately 200 to 300 sepia photographs mainly of back streets in Derby and its suburbs, but also several of the outlying Derbyshire villages. His studio was at 210 Abbey Street between the Old Spa Inn and Thomas Bell, the shopkeeper. The first two photographs of this introduction are typical of his fine work.

These few social history scenes are just a taste of many to come from Derby's professional and amateur photographers, as like the Mayor and his Coachman we take a trip around Derby's roads and also its back streets.

On this trip we also learn of the many influential industrial and business pioneers of Derby such as Michael Thomas Bass, Henry Boden and Sir Francis Ley, as well as the smaller businessmen with their corner shops, who played just as important part in the town's prosperity.

Three important members of the Derby 'Buffs', pictured in 1920. The Royal Antediluvian Order of Buffaloes (RAOB) had several lodges in Derby.

Around the Town

Many changes have occurred to Derby's infrastructure since this interesting *c.*1912 view of Derby was taken from the Moreledge Shot Tower looking north. In the immediate foreground lies Derwent Street containing the Market Chambers, John Thomas White & Sons wholesale confectioners and W.G.Brown corn merchants on the corner of Burghley Street. Looking carefully to the left of centre, the gabled buildings on Full Street are discernible. Many famous landmarks are in view: All Saints', St Mary's, St Alkmund's, the Power Station, Silk Mill and St Mary's Bridge.

This busy Cornmarket scene in 1906 has handcarts, tram and hansom cabs. The man on the right is pulling a Stead & Simpson advertising hoarding, mounted on a hand cart outside Salmon & Gluckstein's tobacconist shop, which boasted they were the 'largest and the cheapest'. The fine Tudor style timbering of the Old Angel public house is adjacent to the Maypole Dairy Company outlet. The Empress Tea Store Ltd later became Lipton's provisions store.

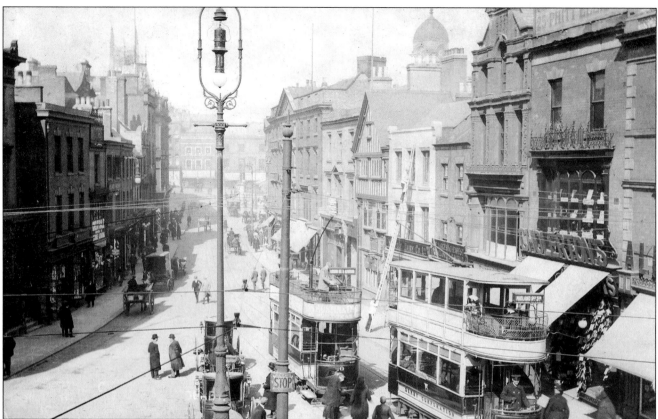

Tram car No.30 makes its way towards the Midland Railway Station as it passes the well-stocked boot and shoe premises of Cholerton's on the Cornmarket where the advertising hoarding announced, 'Phitt Eezie'. The upper floor windows of the Maypole Dairy Company are being cleaned in this 1906 view.

In this early 1930s view, the Cornmarket is extremely busy with a motor bike and side car parked outside the old Midland Railway receiving office (by now the LMS Railway Company). The offices of Derbyshire Farmers Ltd were in the same block. On the right, adjacent to Thomas Smithered the pork butcher, are the prestigious premises of G.A.Dunn & Co Ltd, the famous clothiers and hatters.

Albert House dominates the corner of the Cornmarket and Albert Street and was the home of Robert Jefferson & Sons, the drapers. This *c*.1904 view has captured a heavily-loaded carriage and three-horse team outside Cholerton's shoe shop.

This superb black and white timbered 17th-century building of the Old Bell Hotel, situated on Sadler Gate, was taken by J.R.Board of Buxton in *c*.1930. Fine red port was on offer at 6d a glass, together with a popular price for oysters picked fresh from the beds each morning at 3s for 1oz. The mock Tudor timbering was added as part of the refurbishment carried out by the Derby firm of Messrs Ford & Weston in 1929. The Meynell family built this fine coaching inn around 1680.

The same photographer, J.R.Board, was also responsible for this detailed photograph of the entrance to the Old Bell bar, showing the ornate carved wooden lintel with bell-shaped lamp illuminating 'ye olde' carving of a drinking scene.

Harry B.Hurst had his photographic material premises at 22/23 Sadler Gate in 1908 and he was also an entertainment provider. This extremely scarce photograph was produced by Hurst & Wallis from their 'electric studio' in Sadler Gate and shows Sugar Day in Derby during 1915. A huge crowd of nearly 50 women and one precocious child are cramming into John William Cheshire's provision shop to obtain their sugar rations during wartime in Derby.

Isaac Mason & Son had their oil and colour premises at 31 Sadler Gate and they supplied everything to make the home beautiful. They are both pictured at the entrance to their shop with their delivery boy complete with handcart which contains a can of boiled oil. Their advertisement stated 'Quality is the test of Cheapness'.

A collector's dream is depicted in this c.1908 view of S.I.Levers Fine Arts shop at 55 Sadler Gate. The right-hand window holds many prints, postcards and crested china together with many glamour images. The Levers Brothers, standing in the shop doorway, were to become one of Derby's premier fine art dealers and publishers as well as gaining a fine reputation as carvers, gilders and picture frame makers.

All shapes and sizes of Derby crested ware are on show in the author's display cabinet. Teapots, urns, shaving mugs, dog etc., were produced by W.H.Goss, Arcadian China (Stoke-on-Trent), Lead-beater China (Longton), Fairy Ware, Willow Art, Florentine China etc., and all were available from the Levers Brothers fine art shop in Sadler Gate.

A few rarer shapes of crested ware such as tank, grandfather clock, table and bowl were also available with the statutory 'Buck in the Park' Derby crest. The centre item was to commemorate George V's Silver Jubilee 1910-1935 and bears the Mayor of Derby's inscription: 'Councillor B.S.Thorpe JP., County Borough of Derby, 5th May 1935'.

Sadler Gate is heavily decorated for the July 1933 royal visit of King George V and Queen Mary, two years prior to their Jubilee. On the immediate left is John Lightfoot's family butcher's shop (later Melia's Ltd) with the Strand Arcade in the distant left. The Shakespeare Inn is on the right-hand side with the Animal Hospital in the middle right.

NNU 127 the highly-polished van belonging to C.A.Newton & Co Ltd is obviously on a repair trip in the late 1920s. They were electrical engineers based at 19 St James's Street and specialised in AGA storage cookers and water heaters.

Bass and Worthington were the order of the day at the St James Hotel managed by Fred Mander at the time of this 1910 view. This is the entrance off St James's Street with the decorative awning and Commercial Room to the left and the Sitting Room to the right. The façade is now all shop-fronted.

An earlier *c.*1905 view shows the entrance on the corner of St James's Street and the Cornmarket where a policeman appears to be on point duty. Good stabling, garage and large lofty bedrooms were advertised here. The St James Hotel was originally built in 1866 to designs by Giles & Brookhouse.

A *c.*1905 interior view of the well-appointed dining room of the St James Hotel where excellent cuisine and wines were served.

In 1904 Henry Francis had his hairdressing premises at 8 St James's Street, and by 1906 James Swallow had taken it over after leaving Bond Street in London. This view must be soon after the transfer because Francis's name signs are still evident. James Swallow had won exhibition diplomas in both London and Paris for his specialist work. He was the inventor and sole manufacturer of Derwent Transformation and Toupees.

This interior view shows Swallow's Fancy Sales department where a great variety of toilet requisites of the best quality were available.

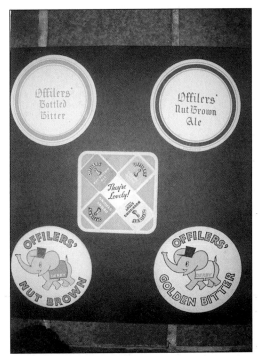

A further selection from the Offiler's range including an advertising pack of cards where the judge has 'just *tried* a bottle of Offiler's Bitter', a pocket-size pale brandy bottle and art deco porcelain dish for change.

How many local Derbeians can remember seeing pink elephants when drinking Offiler's ales? Here is a selection from Offiler's colourful range of beer mats, advertising their Golden Bitter and Nut Brown Ale.

Offiler's produced this novelty tie-on ticket to ensure their drinkers got home safely! George Offiler of the Vine Inn in Whittaker Street was the pioneer. Offiler's sold out to Bass in 1966.

I'm out for the Day and Night!

IF I GET DRUNK
Tie this Label to my Button Hole and

Send me Home

Name _____

Address _____

Do not knock, ring the Bell,
and when the Missus comes run like **L**

(ISSUED BY OFFILERS' BREWERY LIMITED)

The old Shot Tower dominates this early 1930s view of the corner of Albert Street and the Morledge. The tower, built in 1809 by Joseph Gascoyne, disappeared in 1932 to allow the building of the present Corporation Street.

The Exchange Hotel sold Offiler's Ales from 1920 onwards and Fred Parkin Mills was in charge here, adjacent to E.C.Breed's Billiards Saloon on the right. The wooden building opposite appears to be a forerunner to 'Uncle Tom's' tea cabin. The Exchange Hotel took its name from the nearby Corn Exchange and originates from c.1862.

This colourful art deco style artist's impression of the interior of the Palais de Danse shows the sheer luxury of the decor and lighting. Private dancing lessons were available daily and two jazz bands were on hand. It housed luxurious lounges, tea and supper rooms until the *Derby Evening Telegraph* took it over as offices in 1929.

The old Corn Exchange building of 1862 became the Palace Theatre of Varieties in 1897, and in this 1908 view Thomas Edwards was the licensee and manager. The adjacent building in Exchange Street is part of the Exchange Buildings housing Arthur Paxton, collector of taxes. Dancing here was advertised as 'twice nightly', although this was actually 3pm to 6pm at 1s 6d and 7.30 to 11pm at 2s 6d. A special night every Friday cost 5s with evening dress essential. Dancing partners could be supplied on request until the dance hall's closure in 1914 upon the outbreak of war.

After World War One, the Palace of Varieties became the popular Palais de Danse, opening in 1919. Advertised either side of the stepped entrance is their Grand Carnival Novelty Dance, Popular Night and Tea Dance. The motor vehicles on the right belong to John Radford, provisions merchant, adjacent to the Derby Provident Society Ltd. Yeoman's the tobacconists have recently opened a new branch on the left, close to the Trent Motor Traction Co Ltd's motor omnibus depot in this 1920s view down Albert Street.

Thomas Edward Yeoman opened his tobacconist's business on the west side of Derby Market Place (left) during the 1880s, and by the mid-1890s he had further shops in St Peter's Street (centre) and Midland Road (right). The three views shown here were taken in 1906, by which time he also had shops in Ilkeston and Matlock.

The business expanded rapidly after World War One and T.E.Yeoman & Sons (1921) Ltd established further premises in the Cornmarket, Albert Street (stores), Sadler Gate, the Wardwick and Pear Tree Road together with kiosks in the Morledge. Their wholesale business was in Albert Street.

Derby Guildhall is heavily adorned with bunting, flags and the Prince of Wales feathers in readiness for the Royal Visit of the Prince and Princess of Wales on 17 December 1872. This early photograph was by the notable photographer Richard Keene (1825-1894).

The impressive large traction engine complete with cart belonged to A.T.Wigdon of Derby. The exact occasion and location is unknown. The gathering is predominantly the working class of the period which is thought to be *c.*1890s. Some of the group closest to the compound engine could belong to some kind of travelling fair. However the Union Flags in the cart suggest a possible royal or patriotic occasion.

Derby Market Place was motorist friendly at the time of this late-1930s view when a motor park existed in front of the Guildhall. Cantor's furniture store, to the right of the picture, has now disappeared and the building has become yet another city centre bar and eaterie, this time named the Jackie Stamps as a tribute to the great Rams player of the 1940s.

This mid-1920s view records the outline of Derwent Street off the Market Place and also that the Market Place has a commercial purpose. The canvas coverings just beyond the cars belong to Johnsons Brothers & Co Ltd, fruiterers and wholesale banana merchants.

Derby's war memorial was unveiled on 11 November 1924 by Alderman Oswald Ling. The following is a list of the buildings in the background of this c.1925 view, from left to right: W.Kay & Sons, seed merchants; John Jones & Sons, cabinet makers and house furnishers (note the sign for the Derby Vacuum Cleaner); Pountain & Co. Ltd, wine and spirit merchants; and just in view, Isaac Macbeth, antique furniture dealer.

These Assembly Rooms were built in 1763 by Joseph Pickford to designs by Earl Ferrers. They were demolished in 1972 after an earlier fire and the façade was re-erected at the Crich Tramway Museum.

The Assembly Rooms provided a variety of entertainment and function facilities to the people of Derby. This 12-man line-up is the popular Bees Dance Band who in the 1920s provided the music to waltz, foxtrot, two-step and valetta.

The Bemrose Litho (Printers) Dance Club Carnival was held at the Assembly Rooms on 3 April 1925 and the bee symbol denotes that the Bees Dance Band would be in action that night. Mr M.Peckwood was the honorary secretary and MC for the evening.

Fine art dealers Lever Brothers published this unusual Whit Tuesday view of Children's Day celebrations in Derby Market Place in 1905.

About 50 firemen, two policemen and 50 special constables stand to attention behind the Mayor of Derby and other dignitaries. The portion of the Market Place from Carter's glass and china showrooms at the left of the Market Head, past J. & G.Haywood's ironmongers, the Wine Vaults pub, through to Philip Wood's corn merchant's store is dominated by the presence of approximately 400 men. Note the premises of Charles Barrow Keene, the photographic apparatus dealer of 18 Market Place. The Mayor is Alderman Joseph Hill, so the year must be 1914, the start of World War One.

Outside the *Derbyshire Advertiser* office, four copies of the newspaper's 1911 George V Coronation edition are displayed and the buildings all carry regal emblems. Yet what appears to be a long mourning parade silently pass the front of the Guildhall. The Derby and Derbyshire Automobile Club were responsible for the fixing of road signs during this period.

The Mayor of Derby stands aloft on the tank sited in the Market Place as part of the 'Buy War Bonds' campaign in 1915. The banner hanging behind refers to National Tank Week and fund raising Tank No.119 was later to visit Nottingham for a similar National Savings event.

Over 50 local dignitaries are on the makeshift platform erected in front of the Police Station in 1910 as, to a fanfare of trumpets, the Mayor of Derby, Sir Henry Howe Bemrose, proclaims the accession to the throne of King George V. Standing second left to the Mayor is the Rt Hon Lord Roe, who in this year was to be appointed Mayor of Derby for a third term.

The mock Tudor-fronted Horse and Trumpet public house in this early 1960s view was a rebuild carried out in 1928 by Offiler's Brewery. The original 18th-century building on Full Street was in the 1920s owned by Pountains of the Market Place. The neat island is on Corporation Street.

Thirteen neat circles of floating lily leaves, four potted shrubs and two turtles will be forever in many local people's memories from their visits to Derby's famous River Gardens. The gardens were laid out and opened to the public in 1934. This is an early 1950s view and the Derby Hide, Skin, Fat & Wool Market near the Cattle Market is just out of sight above the steps. The large lily and fish pond was known as the 'Grand Canal' but it has long disappeared and the turtles are now at Allestree Park.

A familiar Derby c.1904 panoramic view taken from the Derwent Bridge. Eastwood's tannery lies to the left on Full Street with the Derwent c

These two early-1930s photographs were titled *Derwent-side* and both views are looking from St Mary's Bridge towards the Market Place. A close-up of the barge shows the strange wooden cupboard at the stern together with large oars. Three men are aboard the old barge on the Derwent close to the low weir across this stretch.

ks of W. & J.Lowe to the right of the Silk Mill. The large timber stacks and store to the right belonged to Graham & Bennett on Derwent Street.

The Silk Mill was completed in 1721 by John & Thomas Lombe and their engineer, George Sorocold. Using the River Derwent for power and with sophisticated machinery they placed Derby at the forefront of silk production for many years until it ceased in 1890. By 1891 the structure of the Silk Mill had deteriorated into a poor state and was threatened with demolition. This important photograph records the great fire on 5 December 1910 when the mill was all but destroyed.

Far left: At the time of the Silk Mill fire, F.W. Hampshire & Co were *in situ* here, having taken over from the English Sewing & Cotton Co in 1908. The Silk Mill was eventually rebuilt but reduced to three tiers. This photograph shows the burnt-out shell the day after the fire. For some years it remained empty until the electricity utility used it for workshops and storage until the present-day Industrial Museum brought it back to life on 29 November 1974.

Left: Two elderly Derbeians have come to survey the damage. The magnificent gates produced by Robert Bakewell stand intact after the fire.

A photograph taken in *c.*1906 shows the large expanse of water at Nun's Mill. Francis Agard of Ockbrook, and John Rawlins once owned the ancient Nun's Mill when it had a function with the manufacturing of silk and narrow tapes. Mackworth Road and Merchant Street were built over Markeaton Brook and Nun's Mill Race.

A 1912 view looking up Full Street towards the original Silk Mill public house on the corner of Silk Mill Lane. The left-hand lane is that of Amen Alley, while on the right stands the Corinthian-style Devonshire Alms Houses (hospital) rebuilt in 1778 by Pickford and demolished in 1920 in readiness for the erection of Derby Power Station.

The Royal Standard pub stands at 1 Derwent Street, on the corner of Exeter Place. In this 1935 photograph it seems quite strange to see an 'open plan' bar within the lounge area. George H.Baker was the proprietor at this time when the pub was known as the 'Aquarium House'. Apparently it was a treat to see the fish fed at 8.30 every Sunday night. Offiler's Ales and Pountain's choice wines and spirits were on offer and a spacious club room was available. The RAOB Liversage Lodge would meet here.

PC 228 composes himself to enable Joseph W.Price, the Babington Lane photographer, to produce his portrait in the 1890s. Joseph Price was also an artist and could produce this or any other portrait in oil or water colours to order.

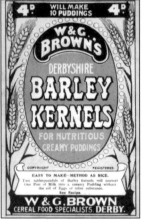

W. & G.Brown were corn merchants on Derwent Street near Nottingham Road, and also had premises on Lodge Lane and Edward Street. They were famous for their barley kernels for making creamy puddings, and allegedly they were a preventative against kidney trouble. A fourpenny packet that would make ten puddings seems excellent value.

The flood water has clearly risen above the Morledge market stalls' counters in this amateur photographer's view of the last great Derby flood in May 1932, looking towards Tenant Street. The advertising hoardings on the left hide the entrance to Thorntree Lane with the White Horse and Noah's Ark public houses just beyond.

Just beyond Derby's prestigious new art deco style Bus Station lies the Cattle Market pens. The Bus Station was completed in May 1933. The curved building left, behind the railing, was the Market's Office in this *c.*1935 view. The Corproation Hotel stands to the right of the cattle pens and closed in 1970. The Bus Station was planned for demolition in 1998.

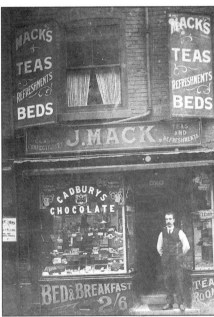

Henry Bostock, his wife and daughter pose for the photographer outside their tobacconist's shop at 3 Cockpit Hill during the period celebrating King George V's Coronation in 1911. Many types of cigarettes were available here including Three Castles, Mitchell's Golden Dawn and F. & J.Smiths Wild Geranium and Regimental cigarettes. Also at this address were Charles Hastings Hirons, saw repairer, and Owen Roberts, woodturner.

The Derby Angling Association was an institution whose honorary secretary was Mr George Eley of the Boat Tavern on Cockpit Hill. The Boat Tavern was classed as a beerhouse only at this time, having lost its status as a tavern some-time between 1846 and 1888, where previously it had been known as the Old Boat on the Morledge. In 1906 at least 30 other clubs were affiliated to the DAA. This proud man was the winner of the association's cup in 1909.

John Mack, complete with pipe, poses for the photographer in this *c.*1912 view of his shop and dining rooms situated at Tenant Street, next door but one to the corner of the old Market Street. Mrs Mack can be seen peeping out of the upper window, and it was she who played a major part in the refreshments and bed and 'breakfast for 2s 6d' facilities on offer at Mack's dining rooms. During the late 1920s Francis J.Mack was recorded as the dining room proprietor.

Ernest Townsend, the talented Derby artist, painted this fine view of the Town Clerk's offices often referred to as the Mayor's Parlour. It was built *c.*1489 and this grand timber-framed house with five gables was swept away for no good reason in 1948. Ernest Townsend's fine brush works depicts Chelsea Pensioners. Mr Townsend was for some time situated in the All Saints' Chambers in Irongate and was later listed at 31 Full Street.

COUNTY BOROUGH OF DERBY

BYELAW FOR THE GOOD RULE AND GOVERNMENT OF THE COUNTY BOROUGH OF DERBY and for the prevention of nuisances made by the Council of the Borough in pursuance of Section 249 of the Local Government Act, 1933, at a meeting of the Council held on the 7th day of December, 1949.

(1) It shall be an offence to offer a contraceptive for sale by means of an automatic machine so placed that it can be used by persons who are in a street.

(2) In this byelaw the expression "street" includes a way or place over which the public have a right of passage, and also the forecourt of or entrance to a building, provided that such a forecourt or entrance is exposed to the view of persons passing along the street, and that the public have unrestricted access to such forecourt or entrance.

(3) Any person offending against this byelaw shall be liable on summary conviction to a fine not exceeding five pounds and in the case of a continuing offence a further fine not exceeding forty shillings for each day during which the offence continues after conviction therefor.

SEALED with the Common Seal of the within-named Mayor Aldermen and Burgesses of The Borough of Derby by Order and direction of the Council of the said Borough this 2nd day of March, 1950.

C.S.

Signed : E. H. NICHOLS,
Town Clerk.

I hereby confirm the foregoing byelaw and fix the date on which it is to come into operation as the date hereof.

Signed : J. CHUTER EDE,
One of His Majesty's Principal Secretaries of State.

Seal of the Secretary of State.

Whitehall,
6th June, 1950.

A sign of the times when 48 years ago, a Derby Borough byelaw meant you could face a fine for selling a commodity now on open sale without any stigma attached.

Several road workers with their large shovels, forks and brushes proudly pose for the photographers from Herbert Parker's of 63 London Road. Invicta No.9 stream roller is to the right of this *c.*1930s photograph.

During World War Two, many local Derby women did their bit for the war effort by carrying out various duties when many male employees were called up for military service. These six young ladies are wearing the smart uniforms of the Derby Corporation Electricity Department, where they were employed as meter readers during October 1940.

Ethel Jackson, daughter of Charles Jackson whose grocery shop was on the corner of Union Street and Traffic Street, is somewhere in this 1915 view of Class Six belonging to Traffic Street's Council School. Just one short of 40 pupils, this group of 18 girls and 21 boys have quite an array of flowers in front of them.

Dora Stead looks to be the perfect Flower Queen in the Floral Festival held in 1912 by the Primitive Methodist Sunday School on Traffic Street.

These four young children have just sampled the delights of the sweet shop on Traffic Street in 1911. Here you were assured of a good and varied window display of Fry's and Rowntree products. This shop was a noted stopping point when on the way to the Coliseum. The Traffic Street area suffered heavy demolition when all was swept away in 1931 for road widening.

John Astle of the Derbyshire Farmer's can be seen here with one of the delivery vehicles, NU 7759, during the 1930s.

This 1906 view is of Frank Porter's removal contractor's premises in Traffic Street on the corner of Liversage Place, a business which commenced at the turn of the century. The depository was spacious and heated throughout for warehousing customers' furniture. Porter's also had premises in Normanton Road and Upper Dale Road, but by the 1920s they were situated on London Road, and also in East Street by the 1930s. Even in this early Edwardian view they advertised 'special low rates for Continental removals'.

The dairy farmer in the loft is piling cheeses c.1932, ready to be loaded into the old Dennis vehicle just in view on the right. Milk and cheese were plentiful at the Derbyshire Farmers Ltd dairy situated on Traffic Street. Their main office was at 19 the Cornmarket where C.G.Swift was the secretary. They also had branches at Ashbourne and Willington. Mr J.L.Thompson was the manager. The Traffic Street establishment later became known as Hadfield Dairies.

Note the spare tyre on the roof front of the Derbyshire Farmers Ltd vehicle for delivering their pasteurised milk, prime cheese, fresh dairy butter and cream. This photograph was taken on one of their deliveries to Willington in the 1930s.

All Saints' Post Office is just beyond the Dolphin in this 1907 view by photographer Charles W. Lee, looking down Queen Street into Irongate. Mrs Annie Porter's bakery shop is on the middle right at 44 Queen Street.

The Derby Corset Depot dominates the east corner of Irongate with the Market Place (old Market Head) where James Swan was listed as the 'Fancy draper' in 1908. On the west side beyond the entrance to Sadler Gate lies Tom Taft's the Globe wines and spirits vaults with Thomas Dean's Robin Hood Inn beyond Chas Foulds music warehouse.

The tram lines do not appear to be *in situ* in this *c.*1904 view looking up Irongate towards All Saints'. On the west side just below Crompton & Evans Union Bank stands the dining rooms of William James Clarke where 'hot dinners are available daily'.

Two wilting chrysanthemums and several other vases of flowers adorn the Children's Corner of Derby Cathedral in this *c.*1929 interior view. This corner vanished in 1972 when the cathedral was extended. However, the grand cupboard has been re-sited.

Both Cox & Bowring and Pountains were wines and spirits merchants who claimed 1763 as the year of their establishment. This 1906 view is of Cox & Bowring's head office and cellars with one of their delivery vehicles in Irongate close to Amen Alley. They were blenders of the noted 'White Seal' ten-year-old whisky. The Coxes were prolific wines and spirits merchants with Cox & Malin in the Cornmarket and Cockpit Hill, Cox, Haden & Pountain wines and brandy merchants in the Market Place where Henry and William Cox were the leading lights during the first half of the 19th century. This curved façade later became the Irongate Tavern and later still was renamed a number of times. In 1998 it was announced that the premises would become a 'Mediterranean-style' bar.

1634 was the year that this fine bell-shaped mortar for Cope & Taylor, the Derby chemists, was manufactured by Heathcote of Chesterfield.

The Southwell diocese, created in 1884, was eventually split and the Derby Diocese came into existence on 7 July 1927 when All Saints' Church was officially elevated to Cathedral status. Derby's first Bishop was Dr Edmund Courtney Pearce who was enthroned by the Archbishop of Canterbury, Dr Hardcastle, on 29 October 1927. He was a former master of Corpus Christi College, Cambridge, and remained at Derby Cathedral until he was succeeded by Dr Alfred Rawlinson in 1936.

Two portraits, including one with full bishop's mitre, are of the second Bishop of Derby, the Rt Revd Alfred Edward John Rawlinson who remained in office from 1936 to 1959.

PADLEY
Chapel of the Martyrs

This view from the same series as those previous depicts the incredibly ornate Pieta Chapel within St Mary's Church.

St Mary's produced this special card to commemorate the death of the Rt Revd Monsignor Charles Payne on 19 December 1944. He had faithfully served St Mary's for many years.

An unusual view of St Mary's Catholic Church, taken from the rear garden, is shown here in this 1930s view with the spire of St Alkmund's adjacent. The Bridge Gate church was erected in 1838 to a design by Pugin. The church was enlarged and beautified in 1853 and provided seating for 550 worshippers. A convent for Sisters of Mercy and a high school adjoined the church. The tower was restored in 1927-28 and a statue of the Blessed Virgin placed on top of the tower.

Bath Street used to run from Well Street to River Street and in this photograph many locals have turned out to witness the 1908 well dressing celebrations. The well can be seen in the distant left. Only three men are in this interesting example of local social history, which is dominated by women and young girls. Bath Street has a long established relationship with the textile industry and the following businesses were situated here: Derby Cotton Mill Co (winders and doublers); George Holme & Co (worsted cloth manufactures); Hargreaves, Madan & Ireland (shoe & slipper manufacturers); and the Derby Weaving Co (cotton). The message on the rear of this photographic postcard reads: 'Dear M, Arrived here alright 4.15. It is very rough here but fine. None of them knew me. They do talk funny, I have got such a job to understand.' It was addressed to Southampton.

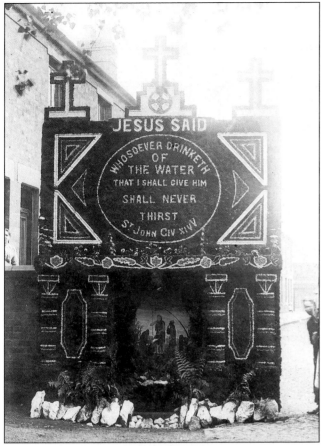

Forty-five girls made up Group 1 of St Alkmund's School in this *c.*1908 view. St Alkmund's Public Elementary School was situated on Edward Street close to North Parade, adjacent to W. & G.Brown's oatmeal mills. The school was erected in 1852, for 188 girls and 167 infants. Miss K.Middleton was the infants, mistress, and Miss S.Badderley the girls, mistress. Boys eventually were taught here and Sarah Badderley gave long service into the late 1930s.

The dressing of St Alkmund Well took place on Ascension Day. The Bath Street well dressing, revived in 1870 and much larger than most and intricate in design, was made from buttercups, daisies, grasses etc., placed on a timber superstructure over the well and taking many hours to complete. Rivermead House flats now overshadows this site.

Forty-five members and nearly 45 smiles from St Alkmund's Church Mission Band in 1938. The captain of the Church Army here at this time was Captain Emanuel, front row fourth from the left.

This photograph was sent to Jefferson County, Colorado, USA, in 1907 and shows the grand interior of King Street Wesleyan Chapel. The chapel was situated on the opposite corner of Chapel Street to the New Flower Pot public house. The Revd Walter Charlesworth (superintendent) and Revd Harold C.Morton used to make their way up the staircase to deliver their sermons to the King Street circuit at the carved pulpit.

The Revd Harold C.Morton is pictured here in 1907, back row left along with his Wesleyan colleagues of the King Street circuit, Revd W. Charlesworth, Revd Harry Swanborough and Revd William Unsworth.

Seventeen non-players and 12 players form this view of the King Street Institute members taken in 1913. The photograph was sent to Bro Holmes at 76 Meynell Street in December 1913 with the message: 'The class will not meet tonight.' The sender was fellow Wesleyan, Percy Pask.

This photograph depicts 21 members of the Derby United Evangelists in c.1910. Back row (left to right): C.Shepperd, Charlie R.Morton, J.Clarke, A.Scotton (honorary secretary), C.Stainfield, E.A.Bush and J.Humphrey. Middle: W.Edge, E.P.Piercey, A.Myers (treasurer) A.W.Rudge (leader), C.L.Flower (assistant leader), W.Mundy, W.D.Rees. Front: E.Bexsan, W.Peake, W.Kirkman, C.Bentley, S.R.Poole, W.Trowbridge, A.Seal.

In 1862, Derby Corporation purchased St Helen's, the former residence of Lord Belper, to house Derby School. In 1872 additional rooms were added in commemoration of the visit paid to the school by the Prince and Princess of Wales (later Edward VII and Queen Alexandra). A handsome chapel was added in 1893 and the school playing fields extended to 13 acres. Derby School produced many eminent scholars including John Flamstead MA, the first Astronomer Royal, and Sir John Eardley Willmott Kt, Chief Justice of the Common Pleas.

The gaslit science laboratories at Derby School were built in 1893, at the same time that the chapel was added.

This photographic montage contains an incredible 18 views of mainly sporting achievements at Derby School in 1932 together with two views of their play *Richard II*. Some of the athletic stars of that year were Pennington, Lorimer and Moon. The house football, cross country and hockey team successes are also featured.

Seventy-six junior and senior school members, together with staff, form this 1912 photograph down by the River Derwent. Several of the Derby School members were extremely keen rowers. Derby Rowing Club and the Derby Town club joined together in 1903.

Only two players are sporting their school soccer crests in this view of Derby School's first team during the 1926-27 season.

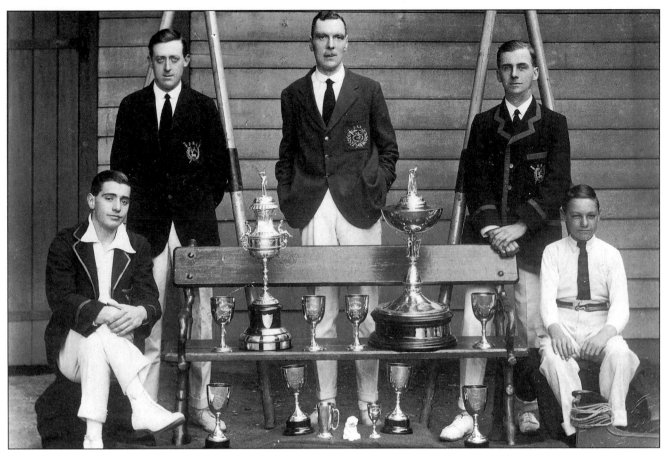

Several trophies and cups are placed on display by the junior crew of the Derby Rowing Club in 1923. The photograph has been signed as follows: R.E.Haywood — Stroke, G.Dickenson — 3, G.Roe — 2, J.W.Harvey — Bow, J.Lawson — Cox. The Derby Rowing Club, formed 1856-57, revived Derby Regatta in 1880.

It is time for a cool mineral water on a hot 1920s Regatta Day on the Derwent. This little wooden tea room complete with verandah was a popular venue for members of Derby Rowing Club and their families.

St Alkmund's and St Mary's Churches stand in the background of this view featuring the cut of the old Derby Canal where boats joined the river to access the mills at Darley Abbey. The reflections of the medieval chapel and the bridge (constructed 1789-94) are captured in this 1933 view.

Frederick J.Boyes, the celebrated Osmaston Road photographer, took this view of a highly-polished, craftsman-built Gospel wagon in c.1911. This newly completed Gospel car is believed to be in the yard of its manufacturer Holmes & Co, the London Road coach and carriage makers.

The old St Mary's Gate House, originally built for the Osbourne family in 1724 and subsequently bought by the Evans family (bankers) in 1777, was converted in 1842 to a Baptist chapel. The General Baptist Chapel stood in a large courtyard entered by a fine stone gateway with elegant wrought-iron gates, designed by Robert Bakewell.

The chapel interior contained much of the former Evans family house mahogany panelling and after conversion it provided 1,200 sittings. Kennings bought the building in 1938 and demolished yet another portion of Derby's heritage. The site is now used as a car park.

This extremely rare view shows where Bold Lane and St Mary's Gate merged together in *c.*1906. To the right stands the Bold Lane Theatre and Gospel Hall (1865) and adjacent various advertisements are displayed for Derby's Grand Theatre and Nottingham's Empire. Richard Ward, the butcher at 12 Bold Lane, stands in the doorway of his shop (formerly John Hay's) with hands on hips in amazement at the large crowd gathered outside the doorway leading to George Winson Mason's Star & Garter Inn at 21 St Mary's Gate. Many women and children are present and each person carries a jug, prompting the possibility of 'free beer' or some other more meaningful reason.

The Chronicle and the *Daily Express* hoardings report the recent North Sea disaster where 65 lives were lost in three shipwrecks while another informs us of the transfer of 'Kelly', and 'British Labour and Russia'. The corner of Willow Row and St Helen's Street was the location for T.W.Boden's hairdresser's and newsagent's shop where a whole plethora of advertising hoardings were in existence in this *c.*1909 view. The shop later came under the control of newsagent Thomas Quigley in the mid to late 1920s.

Arnold Woodhouse, the fruiterer of 30 Willow Row, has specially decorated his shop for the Royal Visit to Derby in 1933. The doorway on the right would have led to the Windmill public house which was shortly to close in 1934. Arnold took over the business from Thomas Cornhill in *c*.1929-30. The Gold Flake and Navy Cut advertisement are those featured in the previous view of the corner newsagent's shop.

A photographer (Renaud), from Chorlton-cum-Hardy believe it or not, took this extremely busy scene above East Street on St Peter's Street in *c*.1907, looking down towards Albert House in Albert Street. The famous Midland Drapery magnet sign is visible and at this time Boots had their premises on the corner of St Peter's Churchyard before moving to the opposite side near East Street. Renaud has captured much activity and debris outside Yeoman's the tobacconist and Jerome & Eugene Deque's dining rooms, possibly the scene of an accident.

It Must Be Love is showing at the White Hall cinema in this Valentine's publication of St Peter's Street. Colleen Moore was starring at the 'Super' cinema as it was known at this time. Boots the Cash Chemists have now moved over to the new decorative building on the East Street corner (1912). The Midland Drapery magnet is much clearer in this 1930 view and reads: 'The Magnet that Draws the People'. The White Hall cinema changed its name to the Odeon in 1935 when Oscar Deutsch took over ownership. It closed as a cinema in May 1965 and British Home Stores took over the site for their new store.

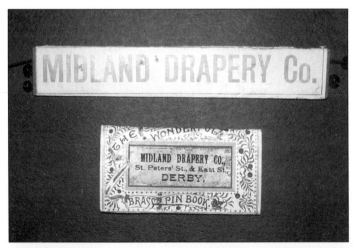

The Midland Drapery advised: 'Ladies should purchase BRASS PINS ONLY. Those described as plated are made of iron and will consequently spoil any material by RUST.' The item at the top houses various sized hat pin needles of the Lewis & Baylis's Cross Fox Brand. 'The Wonderful Midland Drapery Co' used to hand out brass pin books featured below with the inscription: 'Your Change with Thanks.'

The White Hall Cinematography Hall (cinema) boasted a fine cafe-restaurant. Seating for over 50 was provided in grand surroundings with Victorian-style planters and aspidistras. The restaurant opened in 1920 and continued until 1954. The White Hall was built on the former site of the White Swan Hotel and opened in December 1914.

1930s transport dominate the scene in this view looking up St Peter's Street towards The Spot. The old tram tracks are still *in situ* even though the electric trams have now finished. Trolley Bus No.93 was new in October 1932 and this Dobson-bodied vehicle is returning to the depot. This bus was to suffer severe damage in an accident soon after this DSB publication in 1935. It seems quite novel that car YX900 is allowed to park outside the newly opened Marks and Spencer!

A long mourning parade is in progress down St Peter's Street in 1910, shortly after the death of King Edward VII. Easons & Co, the shipping agents, are advertising excursions to Australia and New Zealand as well as Skegness and Mablethorpe. Griffiths & Sons, the watchmakers, and all the other shops on the west side up to the King's Restaurant have ornate hanging bracket lamps to light up their windows.

Progress & Co started as glovers and fancy drapers during the 1890s on St Peter's Street. John Progress remained in business here until *c*.1907. He was an agent for 'Wildspur Lustre Yarns', and the illustration pictured here is a highly collectable advertisement designed by the eccentric cat illustrator, Louis Wain.

This view of the pleasant grassed area with seating close to St Peter's Churchyard was taken shortly prior to the outbreak of World War One. The old Derby Grammar School building which dates back to the 12th-century now forms part of the Derby Heritage Centre. An ugly office block now overlooks this site.

An unusually angled photograph of St Peter's Church taken from St Peter's Churchyard. This church was originally built in the 11th century to Norman and Gothic styles, but extended westward and the tower rebuilt in 1896-1900.

The Grand Clothing Hall Co were tailors in the 1890s, taking over the former draper's premises of John Slack and clothier and pawnbroker George Cholerton in St Peter's Street and remaining here for several decades. The proprietors were Hart & Levy Ltd of Leicester, and besides Derby there were branches in Nottingham and Leicester. The premises were situated adjacent to the Midland Drapery near the East Street corner. 'Oddments under cost,' and 'Bargains in Tunic Shirts,' were advertised during their 21-day sales shown here in late 1930.

This fine view of the street decorations for the 1906 royal visit features the Family & Commercial Derwent Hotel and was published by the Lever Bros of Sadler Gate. The Derwent Hotel was situated at 13 London Road, on the east side at the corner of Devonshire Street. A cold luncheon in Mr A.E.Pollard's establishment cost 1s 6d, and 'Plain & Neat Teas' were also on offer. This commercial hotel was lost as part of the Eagle Centre developments in 1970. The Derwent Hotel was listed in *Bennett's Business Directory* in 1889 as being situated in London Street under the control of newly-appointed proprietor G.N.Ediss, but it dates back to the mid-19th century.

Ernest Elwell was proprietor of the Derwent Hotel at the time of this interior 1935 view of the lounge. As in the earlier view it was a Bass house and bed and breakfast here cost 6s 6d. It was advertised as being situated at The Spot, facing the Gaumont Palace and offering every convenience for the traveller. The Lloyd Loom-style seats and chairs will be remembered by some of Derby's older generation.

The decorated float has just passed the Derwent Hotel and the radio shop of Dalton & Sons at the lower end of London Road, just past The Spot. An accordion player is on board M & D's lorry for what is thought to be a 1940s Hospital Day parade.

The ladder on the left has been put to good use in decorating this narrow cobbled Derby street in readiness for the 1937 Coronation of King George VI. The exact location is unknown but it may have been Eagle Street running from Cockpit Hill to the back of London Road.

G.Gibson & Sons of 92 St Peter's Street were responsible for this superb July 1905 scene of the Lifeboat Procession at the top of St Peter's Street. The crew of the lifeboat are seen prodding the huge crowd with extra long fishing nets in order to collect money. A notice on the lifeboat invites everybody to 'please throw a penny into the lifeboat'. The famous Green Dragon public house has people viewing from windows on all floors of Mr T.Bates's establishment. There were many proprietors of the Green Dragon, both before and after Mr Bates, until its demolition in 1970.

This second view, also by Gibson & Sons, shows the band marching through and several Derby Pierrots can be seen collecting money for the Lifeboat Association.

The white sheet veil is in the process of being removed from the detailed bronze statue of Queen Victoria erected at The Spot. Everybody in the crowd is smiling, from Grace Southern's fruit shop through to Lancaster & Thorpe, the opticians. King Edward VII raises his hat at the unveiling of a permanent memorial to his mother on 28 June 1906. Frank Woore's new and second hand book shop is in the background. In the 1950s and '60s the author can remember spending most of his pocket money on stamps, coins and collectables from Frank Woore's stall in Derby Market Hall when the effervescent and knowledgeable John Archer was in charge for many years.

'The Boot Kings' is displayed above the premises of Freeman, Hardy & Willis, possibly designed specially to coincide with the King's visit. Thousands have gathered at The Spot to cheer the King as he departs for the Royal Show at Osmaston Park on 28 June 1906.

The next Royal Show in Derby was held in 1921, and this special commemorative souvenir biscuit tin was produced with cameo portraits of King George and Queen Mary.

This 1906 interior views tell us that Lancaster & Thorpe's instrument department was upstairs. The decorative cast-iron gas fire was for the comfort of their customers. They had a special sight testing room, and they warned of the danger to the eyes of selecting spectacles from an 'ordinary tradesman's' stock.

An interior view of the workshop where Lancaster & Thorpe manufactured their own spectacles. They advertised that they could do practically any kind of repair, and supply any make of lens the same day as the order was received. We hear of such services now in the 1990s! The man on the right adjacent to the belt-driven grinder was almost certainly wearing his own firm's spectacles.

Lancaster & Thorpe was established in 1887 when Frederic William Lancaster opened his retail and wholesale business at 21 Derwent Street. He was a photographic apparatus manufacturer as well as a spectacle maker. By 1904 he was established at 90 St Peter's Street in partnership with Bertram Samuel Thorpe, a certified optician, and a further branch opened in St James's Street during the early 1930s. Frederic William stands to the right alongside the younger Bertram Samuel Thorpe in this 1906 view of their optician's shop. A large variety of mathematical and scientific instruments were available alongside a wide range of spectacles.

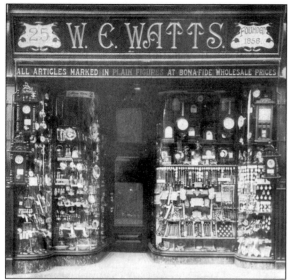

William E.Watts (founded 1858) of 129 Kedleston Road had his prestigious, well-stocked premises at 25 St Peter's Street. He was a watch and clockmaker, goldsmith and jeweller, and he supplied at 'strictly wholesale prices' for cash. He advertised as 'holding the largest stocks of rings in the country' and watch, clock and jewellery repairs were executed on the premises 'with efficiency and promptitude with charges strictly moderate'. Watts' Market Place shop also offered a sight testing and spectacles service conducted by E.Dexter during the early 1930s.

Watts' mahogany cabinets and display cases were craftsman-made and gave the shop an elegant ambience in this 1906 interior view. 'Compare the quality, compare the design, compare the prices, then decide,' was Watts' advertisement. By the 1920s the business was transferred to 9 Market Place and eventually into St James's Street where it still exists as one of Derby's most reputable jewellers. Watts ran their own 'Silver Security Association' and for every 10s paid by subscribers, a bonus of 1s was added.

The Central's book department was the county depot for all educational literature, gift books, prize books, prayer and hymn books etc. Their book room was so arranged that intending purchasers could walk round and inspect the whole of the stock at their leisure and at the time of this photograph included a special show of kindergarten material.

The Central Educational Co Ltd existed on St Peter's Street during the late 1890s as stationers and booksellers. Long-serving William Hart was the early secretary here. Their manufacturing works were on Burghley Street before transferring to Nottingham Road. Their stocks of books were unrivalled for miles around and it was always regarded as a quality shop. The Central also had a large fancy goods department which stocked gifts in silver, electro plate, brass, pewter and leather. The company moved to St Peter's Churchyard in the 1960s but later closed down.

The well-made staircase, display cabinets and neat bookcases just breath quality in this 1906 interior view of the Central Educational's premises.

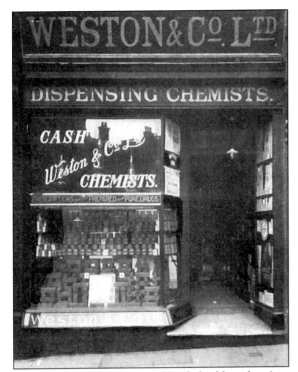

The well-stocked, neat interior of Weston's was lit by ornate hanging globe gas lamps in this *c.*1905 photograph.

Weston & Co Ltd were one of Derby's oldest chemists, situated for many years at 89 St Peter's Street, on the east side. They were high-class dispensing and family chemists.

Established in the 1880s, Samuel Bloor was a saddler and harness maker in East Street where riding saddles and harnesses of every description were made to order. Samuel is standing to the left of his shop entrance in this 1906 view, by which time he had already been awarded five silver medals for superior harnesses and saddlery. Frederick Bloor was also a saddler in the Morledge during 1912, with Frank Bloor a leather merchant on Cockpit Hill during the 1930s.

Admission cost 3d to see the continuous exhibits at the Midland Electric Theatre on Babington Lane. Kinemacolor animated pictures 'in nature's colours' could be viewed only here as the Midland Electric Theatre Co Ltd secured the sole rights for the Midlands. It opened on 27 July 1910, on the site of the former Babington Hall, to designs by Derby architect Arthur Eaton.

'Long live the King' is boldly displayed on the building above Musson & Co's high-class oyster bar, adjacent to Herbert Rose, the tobacconist. The scene is set to celebrate the Coronation of George V in 1911 and Thomas Allen Edwardes, proprietor of the Grand Theatre, and his staff proudly present themselves in front of the circle entrances. Note it cost 8d for a seat in the pit.

R.W.Dudley, photographer of Regent Street, Derby, recorded this intriguing photograph of the 'Giant's' visit to Derby. He is pictured outside the stage door of the Hippodrome in the 1950s and must be almost twice the size of his elderly admirer!

Charles William Lee captured this extremely rare view of the basement dancing academy of Mrs Taft. William Taft was recorded as a dance teacher in Sitwell Street during 1912. The room is heavily adorned with bunting for the royal visit of King Edward VII in June 1906. This particular view is of Taft's 'threepenny hop'. The small centre stage houses piano and violin with William Taft alongside.

The Derby Co-operative Provident Society Ltd's new Merchant Memorial Hall had its official opening on 6 February 1937, when the Society's General Manager, Mr T.A.Peake JP, officiated. This special commemorative booklet was produced for the occasion.

The Co-op's new premises situated at the corner of East Street and Albion Street comprised grocery, provision and butchery departments on the ground floor. The Merchant Memorial Hall and offices were on the first floor with the demonstration and educational rooms on the second floor. The elevations were of a classical design on reconstructed Darley Dale stone, with stainless steel shop fronts with granite surround, while the roof was covered in green West-moreland slates.

Emmanuel Merchant was responsible for the reform of educational work and became the first secretary of the Co-op's Educational Committee in 1898. The Demonstration and Display Hall was equipped with shop windows, counters and fixtures for class instruction in shop window display and salesmanship.

At the time of writing the author has been unable to locate the site of this Derby Co-operative Society shop. Note the height of the manager!

The Derbyshire Permanent Benefit Building Society premises are up for sale on the corner of Green Lane and Victoria Street. The date is clearly May 1932, at the time of Derby's great flood caused by the Markeaton Brook culvert which runs through the centre of the town, being unable to cope with the volume of water. Harry Ranby's shop is on the opposite corner of Green Lane adjacent to the Queen's Head public house where John Renshaw sold Stretton's Derby Ales. The Queen's Head, erected in the mid-18th century, was eventually purchased by Ranby's store (they already possessed 17-24 Victoria Street) and demolished as part of their store re-building in 1961. Eventually the site was acquired by Debenham's.

In 1869, Derby's main postal business centre was transferred from the Royal Hotel building to the Victoria Street Central Post Office. However, this c.1877 view would appear to confirm that the Cornmarket Post Office within the Royal Hotel building was still in use. The Royal Hotel was built in 1838-39 to designs by Robert Wallace. The stove pipe hat and the absence of the horse-tram tracks all help to confirm this photograph to be pre-1880. The hotel's balcony balustrade contains several ornate anthemions together with a fine white Grecian statue. The hotel closed in 1950 and the premises taken over by the DHSS, but part is now converted back to a banqueting suite.

Eighteen men and three ladies comprise the Derby Cycling Club's outing to Burton Woods c.1906. The gentleman standing in the back row, and wearing a bow tie, has a cigarette holder while the man seated from the upper right has two cigarettes in his mouth! They all look very smart and several are sporting their club badges, but where are their bikes?. The HQ of the Derby Cycling Club was at the Royal Hotel on Victoria Street. Cycling was popular and during the 1890s friends of the Wednesday Early Closing Movement formed the Wednesday Cycling Association. Runs were made every week to various parts of the country and their HQ was also at the Royal Hotel Victoria Street.

This Edwardian sporting group is the Derby contingent of the National Clarion Cycling Club meet at Shrewsbury in 1908.

Charles F. Dereske photographed Arthur Chapman on his racing bike in c.1911, complete with his Derby and County Athletic Club vest.

The Victoria Street Congregational Chapel was first founded in 1778 and the building shown here on the corner of Becket Well Lane was erected in 1860 and consisted of chancel, nave, transepts and a tower with spire, and with accommodation for 1,200 worshippers. This late-1950s view shows Ranby's also had premises on the other corner of Becket Well Lane. The Congregational Church was lost as part of the further developments to Ranby's store in 1961-62.

Some of the haberdashery products available from Ranby's drapery warehouse are displayed here. Top: brass pins from the 'Speedwell' range; middle: needles from A.Farr & Sons given out as a change packet. bottom: ½oz packet of hair pins with the inscription, 'Your change with Thanks,' which was the equivalent of one farthing in change.

The first public electric tram car in Derby came into service on 27 July 1904 when a route was opened from London Road to Osmaston Road. Further routes opened between September 1904 and February 1909. This scarce c.1906 photograph is of open-top car No.6 where the destination name board displays 'Victoria Street' (out of view). Only one passenger, lady, is visible.

Victoria Street looks almost empty in this turn of the century view where horse tram tracks are clearly evident. A chink of light on the right denotes Becket Well Lane with John Crooks' boot and shoe dealer's premises on the corner (later Freeman, Hardy & Willis). The Central Post Office and Telegraph Office on the corner of Victoria Street and St James's Street was described as one of the finest buildings in the town.

The young trainer to the right keeps a watchful eye on his 22 youthful Derby telegraph messengers in action on their training ground in 1912. During 1905 the telegraph messengers formed themselves into a cadet corps which was affiliated with the 1st Voluntary Brigade the Sherwood Foresters. The first captain was Postmaster Percy James. In 1892 The Post Office in Victoria Street employed 42 telegraph messengers, and dealt with 800,000 messages delivered throughout the town in the days before everyone had a telephone.

The Victoria Electric Theatre's opening ceremony was officiated by Alderman Thomas Roe. The architect was J.H.Horton who designed seating for 800. Mr F.T.Studd was the first manager of this 'neat up-to-date and luxurious place of amusement in Derby,' where charges ranged from 3d to 1s.

A 1909 view shows an Edwardian picture palace operator at work. The message on the reverse of the photograph tells us that the tweed-suited cine film operator is a Mr Cartledge. He is believed to have been one of the first operators at the Victoria Electric Theatre in Becket Well Lane opposite the General Post Office. The Victoria opened on 10 October 1910 and initially showed silent films in between variety acts.

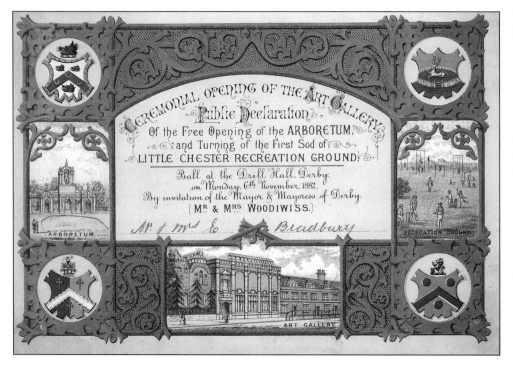

This magnificent chromo-lithographic ornate invitation ticket was sent to Edward Bradbury, the Derby author, and his wife in 1882 by Mr and Mrs Woodiwiss, the Mayor and Mayoress of Derby. The occasion was to celebrate the opening of Derby's new Art Gallery, the turning of the first sod of Little Chester Recreation Ground and the public declaration of the Arboretum becoming free to the public (1882 was a busy year as the Children Hospital's foundation stone was also laid then). To mark the above occasion a grand ball was held at Derby Drill Hall in Becket Street.

Shackleton & Sons were general drapers and carpet drapers on St Peter's Street during the 1880s, moving to the Wardwick at the turn of the century. The household furnishers remained here until demolition in *c.*1912. The gabled building between Shackleton's and the Library belonged to a Dr Fox.

The Central Educational Co Ltd published the following two views of the Jacobean Cafe situated in one of Derby's most historic buildings in the Wardwick. The first view shows the old fireplace in the corner of the oak parlour, while the second shows a further view of the cafe tables

laid out. It was a popular place for morning coffee, luncheon and teas. The house dates from the 17th century and is the oldest brick building in the city.

This Victorian photograph by W.W.Winter's shows Derby's new Free Library and Museum was rebuilt in 1879 in the Domestic Flemish Gothic style. It was the free gift of Michael Thomas Bass MP, of Rangemore, who represented Derby Borough in Parliament for upwards of 35 years. A considerable extension was opened in 1916 consisting of a large reading room on the ground floor and an Art Gallery above.

Probably one of only a handful that may have survived, this important record was a ticket for a very special performance at the Lecture Hall, Derby, on 25 August 1852. The Lecture Hall was a noble and well-proportioned room with a beautiful ornamental ceiling and was part of the Mechanics' Institute in the Wardwick and erected in 1839. The Guild of Literature and Art, with the remarkable Mr Charles Dickens, played *The Frozen Deep* and *Mr Nightingale's Diary.*

The two ornate hanging globe lamps on the left belong to the cabinet maker's premises of Henry Davison, while the horse-drawn delivery vehicle of Derby brewers, Alton & Co, are about to make a delivery to Albert Walkerdine, the beer retailer on the corner of Becket Well Lane. The two young girls on the pavement to the right are close to the amalgamated Friendly Societies Medical Association's base at 29 Macklin Street where several eminent medical officers were in attendance, This 1909 view has an interesting message telling us that Mary lived in the house/apartment on the immediate right; Mary also stated that the new Hippodrome is to be built on the ground between the children and the top of the street, and the houses are being pulled down and the street made wider.

Let's Go is showing at Derby's Hippodrome starring Rorke & Bray, while the following week in 1924 the first-ever stage production of the *1924 Manhattan Follies* starring Fred Duprez was billed as 'a giant production in 20 bits and pieces'. The Hippodrome opened in 1913 to designs by Derby architect Alexander McPherson. For many years now it has been a bingo hall. On the right corner with Macklin Street stands Thomas Glover's tobacconist's shop.

The Stork Inn was situated on the corner of Macklin Street and Colyear Street, being built some time prior to 1855 when J.Bryan was the first recorded proprietor. This interesting social scene has recorded the Stork Angling Club on one of their regular fishing trips in 1917. Mr Henry Ellis was the long-standing landlord here from the 1880s, with Harry Ellis from 1912 through to the late 1920s, and Albert Wildgoose making a brief appearance in 1904. Only three out of 30 are without moustaches and only one without a tie in this smartly turned-out group. An earlier postcard to Henry Ellis dated 1906 tells us that young Harry was taken to Blackpool to have his hand read by the 'darkies'.

Mr George Samuel Simms, the eminent surgeon and physician, complete with bowler hat, stands at the entrance of his prestigious home, The Hollies, on the corner of Green Lane and St Peter's Churchyard. This 1909 view by Frederick J.Boyes (Osmaston Road) shows Mr Simms' horse cab waiting patiently on Green Hill (now Green Lane). It is difficult to believe that this grand structure is no longer standing.

The east side of the narrow Green Lane has an early car, handcart and pony and trap in the vicinity of Goodall & Co, the house furnishers and cabinet makers. The pony and trap is almost standing adjacent to the Grapes public house. W.W.Winter took this c.1912 scene with several people on the right close to the long barber's pole denoting the premises of Frederick Dickinson, the hairdresser.

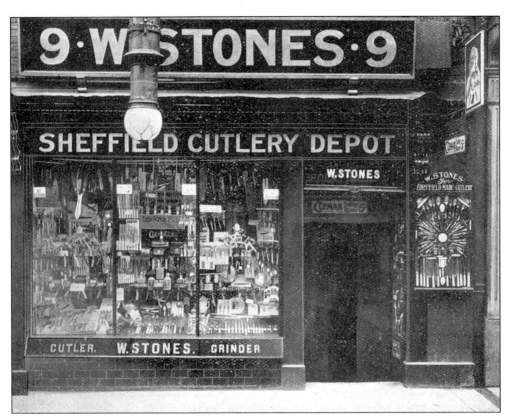

William Stones was a cutter who established his business in Green Lane *c.*1856. All manner of knives, shears and scissors could be bought from his Sheffield Cutlery Depot shown here in 1906 when the business had become W.Stones & Sons. They also specialised in over 50 brands of well-known razors costing from 1s. The 'Special Sharp Razor', complete with box, could be bought for 3s 6d. Situated between Rowley's the florists and the Old Grapes Inn on the east side of Green Lane, Stone's shop remained here for many years.

The multi-gabled Victorian building The Springfield stands at 73 Wilson Street on the corner of Green Lane and was the former home of Alfred Smith, the confectioner and wines and spirits merchant whose premises were on Victoria Street. At one time it was used as a home for under-privileged children.

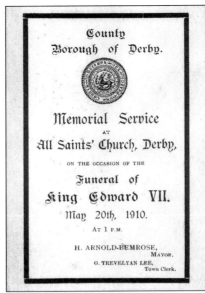

Thomas Rowley & Co were fruit salesmen and artistic florists. This decorative anchor was photographed by Hoar & Sons at Rowley's Green Lane premises in 1910. This was Derby's tribute wreath to be sent for Edward VII's funeral. Rowley's also produced similar special wreaths for the funerals of Queen Victoria and George V. During the 1880s Rowley's well-established premises were listed as 'Covent Garden House, providers of wedding bouquets and English/Foreign fruit salesmen'.

J.W.Simpson & Sons Ltd of Albert Street produced this booklet for the memorial services at All Saints' on the occasion of King Edward VII's funeral on 20 May 1910. The service was conducted by Revd J.Howell, vicar of All Saints' and Revd E.A.Paxton (curate) with the Mayor, H.Arnold Bemrose in attendance.

Simpson's produced a similar booklet for Queen Victoria's funeral on 2 February 1901. The sermon was delivered by the Rt Revd the Lord Bishop of Derby, Dr Were.

A new building in Becket Street to be used as a drill hall by the volunteer corps of Derby was opened in 1870 with a fine arts and industrial exhibition and fancy bazaar. Colonel Wilmot MP, commandant of the volunteers, read the opening address to which the Duke of Devonshire replied. The exhibition included fine pictures, works of art, models of inventions, specimens of nature, antiquarian relics and curiosities.

Military Matters

The Sherwood Foresters' Prisoner-of-War Regimental Care Committee was situated at 21 Park Street, off Traffic Street, and was instrumental in caring for and supporting hundreds of soldiers during the hardships of World War One.

The reverse side tells us that prisoner-of-war Private Gerald Saward of the 2nd Sherwood Foresters, imprisoned in Altmark, Germany, received his army rations of beef stew, dripping,

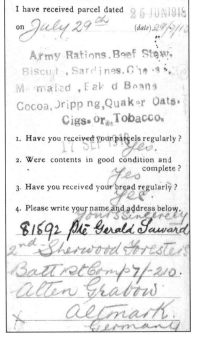

cheese, cigarettes etc., on 29 July 1918, having been posted one month earlier. This card enabled the Care Committee to monitor that their soldiers received regular parcels and that the contents were intact.

This ornate production depicts the Sherwood Foresters' 45th and 95th Foot drummer, ram mascot and colour sergeant. The regiment was formed in 1881 by the amalgamation of the 45th Foot (Nottinghamshire Regiment, raised in 1741) and the 95th Foot (Derbyshire Regiment, raised in 1823).

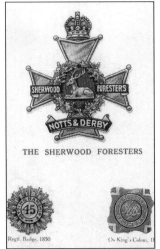

Gale & Polden Ltd produced this as part of their regimental badges series of postcards. The badge crest is a stag within a wreath of oak leaves and was adopted in 1901 and retained until the early 1970s.

Hurst & Wallis produced this photograph from their 'Electric Studio' in Sadler Gate, Derby. It was taken on 13 June 1916, possibly near Normanton Park, and shows Sherwood Foresters at a memorial service for Lord Kitchener, Secretary of War, following his death a week earlier when the cruiser *HMS Hampshire* was struck by a mine and sank without survivors on its way to Russia where Kitchener was to have advised the Tsar on military matters.

The 21-strong brass band, complete with dog mascot, contains at least six Boer War veterans in this 1911 view taken outside the Drill Hall in Newland Street. The drum carries the Sherwood Foresters' badge, the United Red and White Rose.

Raphael Tuck & Sons published this view of a Sherwood Foresters Drum Major as part of their famous 'Oilette' series.

Bacon & Hudson, printers of Colyear Street, produced the Derby Borough Battalion of Home Guards' Weekly Orders for 28 August 1915, containing details of which company would guard the Rolls-Royce factory and the National Shell factory together with firing range and drill details. The complete Home Guards uniform was obtainable from the Capital & Labour Stores, Irongate House, for the princely sum of 22s 6d. The Home Guards were formed on 26 January 1915.

The Newland Street Drill Hall was used for a political meeting on 19 December 1887 where the principle address was delivered by the Marquis of Salisbury KG as denoted in this platform ticket.

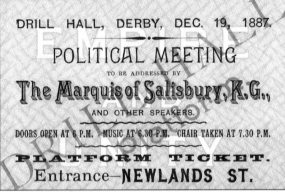

Young and old form the Derby Imperial Veterans' Associations Derby United Prize Band around 1930.

Officers and band of the 2nd Voluntary Battalion of the Notts and Derbyshire Regiment form a 27-strong group in this *c*.1911 view. The ram mascots were all supplied by the Duke of Devonshire from his Chatsworth House farm.

Two hundred and sixty members of 'C' Company of No.10 TB RTC RE are recorded in this July 1940 photograph taken inside Derby County's Baseball Ground.

'Short back and sides' was the order of the day for these 15 young non-smiling Foresters recruits in 'grandad vests'. They appear to be preparing for a training session involving Indian clubs and boxing during 1905.

George Wallis of 135 Watson Street published this *c*.1912 photograph of the 14 members of the Derbyshire Yeomanry at a summer fête held in the grounds of Markeaton Recreation ground off Mackworth Road. In the background the familiar turret of the West End church of St Anne's on Whitecross Street is visible.

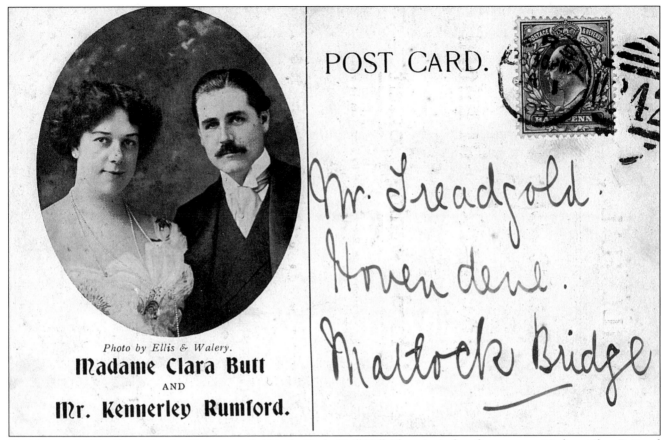

On 4 January 1905, a Grand Evening Concert was held in the Derby Drill Hall. The principal performers were Madame Clara Butt and Mr Kennerley Rumford under the direction of Mr Edgar Horne. Ticket prices ranged from 1s to 6s.

This mug was produced by the Bridge Street Pottery Co, Burslem, as part of their 'Briduria' range. It was on sale in Derby to raise funds for the Fighter Plane Fund during World War Two. Both Derby and Derbyshire produced many fighter pilots of repute including Alan Norman Feary, William Burley Higgins, 'Jock' Wilson, Bill Astell, Cyril Hassell, Harold Hunt, Norman Crookes and Douglas Shepley to name but a few.

Friar Gate & Ashbourne Road

This south view of Friar Gate was taken from the garden of the three-storey 18th-century Friary Hotel. The original 1730s central portion was eventually joined with the right and left wings added in 1769 and 1880 respectively. The former residence of Henry Boden (the lace manufacturer) at 104 Friar Gate, it became the Friary Hotel in 1922 when it was sold to the Whitaker family. The garden is now lost to the building of a modern office block complex.

The wrought-iron arch complete with overhead lamp led to the cobbled area in front of the Grade II listed Friary Hotel.

Friary House School, also known as Friar Gate House School, is situated at 65 Friar Gate on the north side close to Brick Street. It was a day school for girls and preparatory for boys, where Fred Bryan Wibberley was in charge during the 1920s. Note the canary cage on the left-hand table in this somewhat spartan interior view.

From the late Victorian period Belmont House, originally built c.1750 for the Hurt family, was a ladies' school at 99 Friar Gate on the south side close to the GN Railway Bridge, and Miss Louisa Amelia Adams was the long-serving mistress there. The school's objective was 'to educate the girls to form a strong reliant character, which would fit them for any position they may be called to fill'. Belmont afforded ample accommodation for 16 boarders and 56 day girls. Special attention was given to music under the direction of Mr Arthur Francis Smith. In this 1908 scene, Winnie, Mary, Ruth and Minnie take time out on the tennis court.

From their Willow Printing Works on Willow Row (previously Castle Street), Derby Printers Ltd published this political advertisement in 1921 for the Friar Gate Municipal bye-election.

Edmund Charles Clarke & Co were one of Derby's oldest established bicycle and tricycle manufacturers at 1 Friar Gate adjacent to St Werburgh's Church. Clarke's Derby Cycle Works were going strong in the 1880s through to the late 1890s. The Orton Brothers took over here briefly in 1908. Just prior to World War One, cycling became so popular that Derby had over 30 shops selling bicycles.

Horse-drawn vehicles dominate Friar Gate in this *c.*1911 scene. The flat wagons are transporting many barrels, possibly from Stretton's Derby Brewery in Ashbourne Road. On the left stands the premises of the Park Steam Laundry which also had a receiving office in Sadler Gate.

In the centre left is the well-known four-gabled establishment of Copestake & Co, the former Sir John Gell's house of *c.*1643 on the corner with George Street. The long pole out of the third-storey window informs us of the Private Tea Rooms where refreshing ices could be sampled. This view looking towards the Wardwick was published by the Lever Bros, Derby, in 1905.

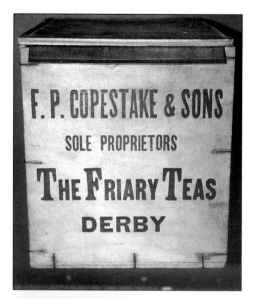

This surviving original wooden tea box, from the author's collection, contained Copestake's propriety brand known as 'Friary Teas'. The box was lined with special thick ribbed paper to prevent dampness.

Handyside's ornate iron bridge carrying the London & North Eastern Railway is in the distance of this 1931 view looking towards Ashbourne Road from Friar Gate. The horse and cart on the right is close to the chemist's shop of Edward J.Readman on the corner with Ford Street. The cyclist has just ridden past the grand former residence of Alderman Cheshyre.

C.W.Lee took this sepia view of several Edwardians out for a stroll on the stretch of Friar Gate running from Bridge Street down to where the GN Railway bridge crosses. Many eminent surgeons and physicians were residents on this north side and the current premises of Breedon Books, the publishers of this book, are in clear view at 44 Friar Gate. The upper end was often called 'the Pussery' because so many 'old maids' lived there! The steps leading to the cobbled high pavement are much the same today.

This elegant sweep of Grade II listed buildings on the north side of Friar Gate between the GNR bridge and Bridge Street have had a chequered career. They were originally built in c.1841 to designs by Joseph Cooper of Derby on the site of the former 1756 County Gaol and have housed a variety of businesses including the Chadfield & Smith School of Music, Friar Gate Commercial Hotel (later The Stamford CH) run by Frederick German, and the Howard Hotel. For a short period the cells underneath, alleged to be haunted, were adapted into Judge Jefferies Bar.

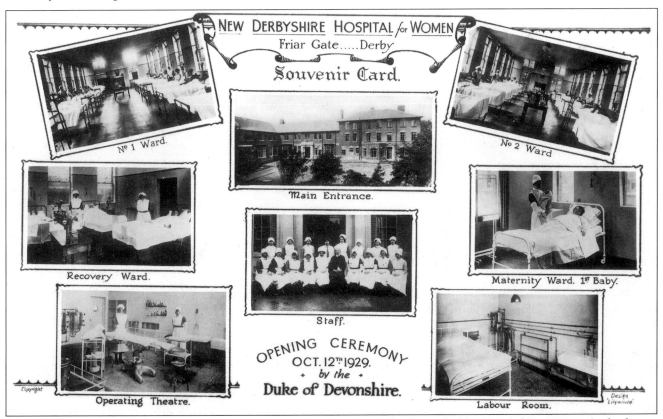

In October 1929 the Duke of Devonshire performed the opening ceremony for the Derbyshire Hospital For Women in the former Wheeldon's House (itself a rebuild of an earlier house) on the corner of Friar Gate and Larges Street. Purchased for a hospital mainly with money from Mrs Mundy of Markeaton and Mrs Evans of Darley Hall, it closed in 1986. One of the eight multi-views features the maternity ward's first baby.

The decorative main entrance to the Royal Institution for Deaf and Dumb was the work of a deaf sculptor. This 1906 view was published by R.Dunn & Co, London, for Derby's Central Educational Co Ltd.

All those who enrolled as a member of the Derbyshire Women's Hospital League (DWH) would have received one of these membership cards.

The deserted south side of Friar Gate in 1918, possibly a Sunday, depicts the Royal Institution for Deaf and Dumb on the raised area just beyond the GNR bridge. The insitution was founded in 1879 and this building was opened in 1894 by the Duchess of Rutland. Two acres of land were attached for recreation at a total cost of £20,000.

The inset portrait is that of Dr William Robert Roe, the headmaster, in this 1906 view. He established a small charity called the Deaf and Dumb Institution at Mount Pleasant in 1873, which was the origin of the Derby Institution.

Dr William Roe and a young boy are pictured in 1908, in the garden associated with the hospital portion of the Royal Institution for Deaf and Dumb.

Below: W.R.Roe personally took the photographs of these happy looking young children during 1910, with rocking horse, skipping ropes and dog. However, a sad message penned to the reverse reads: 'Dear Alice [Boultbee of Normanton Lane, Littleover], I am sorry to tell you little Freddy has died sudden and they are going to bury him on Wednesday so I thought you would like to see the last of him, so be at our house by 1.30pm Wednesday.'

Six of the institution's ladies have sought some shade during the summer of 1907.

'No 1' haircuts were the order of the day for these 50 or so youngsters on the institution's recreation ground. What a cheeky smile from the young Edwardian behind the ball and makeshift goalpost. A baseball bat and gloves are also present on the ground.

William Gillam of Oak's Yard, St Peter's Street, was one of Derby's Victorian photographers and it was he who produced this *c.*1898 view within the interior of Friar Gate Station. This well dressed group were probably part of a Sunday School outing on the Great Northern Railway.

The County Gaol at the end of Vernon Street opened in 1827 at a cost of £65,227 and occupied about six acres. Initially there was accommodation for 315 prisoners, but this was later increased. The Reform Bill Riots of 1831 led to the erection of the eight Martello towers to facilitate defences. It was pronounced by the Society for the Improvement of Prison Discipline to be 'of the best plan and construction in the United Kingdom'. The name changed to HM Prison Derby in c.1886 and the last hanging there took place in 1907. This view was taken in 1904 when the governor was Captain Charles E.Farquherson. It later became Derby Greyhound Stadium, but today only the façade remains leading to an office and housing development.

Situated close to Windmill Hill Lane stood Edward G. Morley's Wagon and Horses public house at the Ashbourne Road tram terminus. This 1908 view shows Mr Morley with his wife and son in the pub's 'continental gardens' where Edwardian customers could enjoy a home-brewed drink at one of the outdoor tables. Derby & County Athletic Club had their HQ here. The pub dates back to c.1833 and the name possibly derived from 'fly wagons' departing from here.

Harry Roger Rolfe, prison chaplain at Derby in 1904, held his position at St Michael's from 1885 to 1925 and eventually became a honorary canon of Southwell and surrogate. Mr Rolfe kept himself busy and was also chairman of the Board of Guardians for the Derby Union Poor Law Offices.

This postcard lists the handicaps for the 70 declared runners taking part in Derby & County Athletic Club's Judge Cup in 1908.

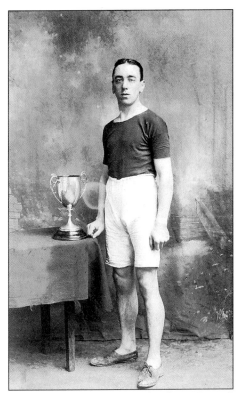

The Derby & CAC ten-mile champion of 1912 proudly poses next to his trophy.

An unknown athlete wearing the D & CAC vest, probably in the 1920s.

This view shows the commencement of the north side of Ashbourne Road from Brick Street. The portly figure of Mr William Farmer is talking to a customer at the entrance to his butcher's shop (previously George Brassington's shop). Two doors further up is the old established pork butcher's premises of George Goodall who was located here along with Brassington's since the 1880s. The pony and cart are parked outside Charles Spalton's corn factory just below the Congregational Church.

The Congregational Church, which provided seating for 350, dominates the north side of Ashbourne Road in 1921. The horse and cart have just passed the left corner with Uttoxeter Old Road. The building was demolished in 1998 after being damaged by fire four years earlier.

The area where Friar Gate becomes Ashbourne Road shows Bridge Street and Brick Street corners to the right and Vernon Street corner to the left.

Charles Bassett Vincent was founder of the Railway Servants' Orphanage, Derby, along with the Amalgamated Society of Railway Servants and the Railway Clerks' Association.

The Railway Servants' Orphanage occupied a six-acre site on Ashbourne Road. Originally a private mansion, the building was adapted and greatly enlarged to open in July 1887. It originally accommodated 272 children, but by 1904, 960 had been admitted. It was demolished in 1982.

On the Friar Gate corner with Vernon Street stood the Diocesan School where Revd Cannon Massey and Fred Adcock were the long-time secretary and headmaster respectively during the late Victorian to c.1912 period. They were succeeded by Revd F.S.Boissier and Corneluis Swanson. At some time after 1935 the principal, Raymond C.Swanson, distributed this illustrated card informing all that the new school's name was Vernon High School. The building later became the 102 Social Club.

Where Friar Gate ends (Uttoxeter Old Road) and Ashbourne Road begins on the south side, you would have found the large premises of Messrs Lucas & Raynes, clothiers and boot and shoe dealers. Although they don't have the familiar three-balls sign, they were also pawnbrokers. James Frederick Raynes was the pawnbroker in the partnership, and both he and Mr Lucas are in this scene along with their assistants. They later opened further premises on Siddals Road.

Twenty-two boys and 21 girls comprise Class Five in this 1910 view of Ashbourne Road School taken at Harvest Festival time. Only one of these infants wears spectacles.

Ashbourne Road Board School was erected in 1879 for 564 boys, 310 girls and 386 infants. The school was enlarged in 1895 for 1,264 mixed and 401 infants. In 1904 the average attendance was 1,274 mixed and 500 infants! The school was situated on the south side near Stretton's Derby Brewery and the Wesleyan Methodist Chapel and School.
Thirty-six cloth caps including boys and masters, form this formidable group from the Ashbourne Road School titled 'The Certificate Boys, 1906'.

John William Thompson lived at 17 Heyworth Street throughout the Edwardian period. This photograph shows J.P.Thompson in the greenhouse of the above address surrounded by his geraniums and ferns in September 1907. The message on the back tells us the greenhouse was built 1904-05.

The Wesleyan Chapel Schools were on the opposite side of Ashbourne Road on the corner with Colville Street in this 1905 view.

The foundation stone to the Wesleyan Chapel on the corner of Ashbourne Road and Surrey Street was laid in 1877. Opened in 1878 to the designs of John Willis of Derby, the chapel was extended in 1885, closed in the early 1980s and demolished in 1986. Stretton's Brewery is noticeable in the background. Note the cobbled pathway across the unmade Surrey Street so as to avoid the mud.

A *c*.1910 view looking down Bass Street towards Windmill Hill Lane. On the right stands St Barnabas's Church on the corner with Radbourne Street. The church was commenced in 1885-86 and completed in 1904 to the Early English style.

'Ring a Ring of Roses' appears to be the name of the game in this pre-World War One view of St John's School in Derby's West End. This public elementary school, situated in Mill Street close to St John's Church, was erected in 1840 and enlarged in 1894 for 357 mixed and 267 infants. W.Henry McCarthy was the master and Miss K.Parker the infants' mistress for several years.

One of the Lever Brothers' publications of 1904 shows the galleried interior of the West End church of St John's. The huge church organ sits high on the left with three large stained-glass memorial windows in the chancel. The message penned on the reverse side is to Mrs Wibberley of 8 Handford Street and reads: 'Meet me at the top of Five Lamps and don't be late, Kit.'

Markeaton Hall, pictured in 1908, sadly now demolished, was originally built in 1755 for Wrightson Mundy to the designs of James Dentstone. Joseph Pickford erected the superb Orangery, which still survives today, and stable block to the left in *c*.1790 for F.N.C.Mundy.

The lady dressed in her black Edwardian finery climbing the terrace steps in 1908 is Mrs Mundy, Derby's 'lady of the manor' whose seat was Markeaton Hall. The Orangery can be glimpsed through the ivy-clad decorative terrace arches. She was born Emily Maria Georgiana Cavendish, became Mrs F.N.Mundy, widowed in 1903 and died in 1929.

This later 1930s view shows Markeaton Hall's neatly laid-out flowerbeds shortly after the grounds became a public park when HRH Prince George the Duke of Kent performed the opening ceremony on 30 June 1931.

Six thirsty horses have been captured in this *c*.1912 view, enjoying a drink in Markeaton Brook.

Three small boys, complete with makeshift rod, are trying their luck with a spot of fishing in Markeaton Brook during 1924.

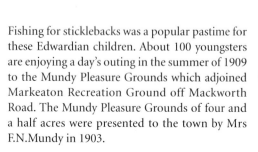

Fishing for sticklebacks was a popular pastime for these Edwardian children. About 100 youngsters are enjoying a day's outing in the summer of 1909 to the Mundy Pleasure Grounds which adjoined Markeaton Recreation Ground off Mackworth Road. The Mundy Pleasure Grounds of four and a half acres were presented to the town by Mrs F.N.Mundy in 1903.

Burton Road

AU 6265 is parked outside Thomas Tooby's stationer's and sub-Post Office on Burton Road, near its junction with Abbey Street in 1929. The other shops in descending order are: Sunnyhill Dairy Ltd; Misses L.E. & E.Segrave, drapers; Mrs Fanny Woods, fruiterer; and Charles Ling, the bootmaker on the corner. The tramline standard on the right looking towards the town centre carries an AA notice: 'Slow Through Derby'.

The man with the white beard appears to be dumping large quantities of bricks adjacent to the tram lines on Burton Road, with several others stacked on the pavement opposite today's Wine Rack shop. This 1908 view depicts the fine gable-fronted Victorian houses on the south side below Breedon Hill Road and Joseph Mason's paint and varnish works.

The Derby Corporation open-top tram has stopped at the tram terminus, on Burton Road, opposite Vicarage Road on the right, in order to take on board several eminent looking people from this exclusive area in 1906. Once the tram track cleaning is finished, this car will make its way to St Peter's Street.

The grand balustraded half-timbered gabled building on the Burton Road corner with Breedon Hill Road was the residence of Charles William Corrie Fletcher, eminent surgeon at the time of this 1913 view. He worked at the Derbyshire Hospital for Women, then on Bridge Street. The Mount Carmel tower belonging to Mason's paint and varnish works, designed by G. Thompson in 1869, dominates the background.

Ye Olde Spa Inn, as it was known here, is a gabled mid-18th-century brick building and was first listed as an inn by the Post Office directory of 1855. *Bagshaw's Gazetteer* of 1846 neither lists Old Spa nor indeed Abbey Street. In 1855 the proprietor was Mr J.Wescott with the Hollis family taking control by the 1880s. William Hollis eventually succeeded to Edward Hollis, who is pictured here with straw boater on the neat lawn at 204 Abbey Street. Edward sold his own home-brewed ales, Walker & Sons' Kilmarnock whisky and a Wright's ten-year-old special toddy. The site of this old inn is associated with Dr William Chauncey's spa of 1733.

'Bennett's Make Keys!' and 'Derby's Key Expert' were the somewhat amateurish advertisements either side of Mrs Bennett outside W.H.Bennett's ironmongers shop some time in the late 1920s. Alex Bennett was to later run this shop and you could still buy anything from a roll of linoleum to a teapot.

William Henry Bennett, pictured with his children, had his General Incandescent Company premises at 11 Abbey Street. It was a wholesale mantle store but all manner of items, from a potato peeler to a sieve, were sold here in this *c*.1909 view. Bennett's was a household name and offered sterling service well into the 1950s.

Six young boys working under the watchful eye of their teacher and only one chair between them. This is an instructional tailoring class at Abbey Street Municipal Boys' School. The centre blackboard confirms the exact date: 'Lesson for 5 October 1910 — The making of a pair of breeches.' The school developed into Bemrose Grammar School on Uttoxeter Road by 1930 and the Abbey Street building became a girl's secondary school before being demolished in the early 1980s.

The bowler-hatted proprietor in this *c.*1908 view of a Derby butcher's premises stands proudly surrounded by carcasses hanging from every available point. The message on the reverse side, to Mr Albert Bowler of 32 Abbey Street, reads: 'Dear Albert, sorry I did not see you Monday night, had another little job on!' The horse-drawn cart belongs to Joseph Harvey of Derby Market Hall.

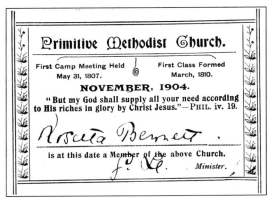

The minister's signature on this Primitive Methodist Church membership ticket is that of Revd George E.Lloyd who administrated the Second Circuit covering Kedleston Street, Mansfield Street and Campion Street churches.

Seven boys and 13 girls comprise this class from the Primitive Methodist Church class on Campion Street. Rosetta Bennett (of Bennett's the ironmonger) is in this group.

This well-built detached house was photographed at 51 Empress Road during September 1912. Belmont and Claremont residences exist nearby before the little jitty running to the right of this house down to Mount Carmel Street and Steps.

The trees lining the north-west and south-east side of Vicarage Avenue are still young in this 1909 view looking towards Burton Road from the direction of Stonehill Road. Many gabled, bay-windowed sturdy Victorian houses exist here with such names as Old Mattonia (north-west side), and Kirkstead, Southbank (south-east side). The hatted Edwardian girl is standing outside No.33 which was the residence of Albert Edward Brindley MD, Medical Officer of Health working out of Ford Street Derby. David S.Butler, the renowned Derby stationer and publisher, lived at No.22 for several years.

This unusual c.1909 view is looking up Whittaker Road towards the old turreted house on the corner of Burton Road and Vicarage Avenue. The boy standing on the corner with Overdale Road appears to be delivering newspapers. All the right-hand houses with their sturdy bay-windows had names: The Uplands, Berwen House, Chislehurst, Lyndhurst, Strathyre and Allestree, and local business people resided here.

The ornate railings and decorative greenhouse on the right corner belonged to 17 Avondale Road in this 1909 view looking towards Renals Street from Mill Hill Lane. No.17 was the home of several years to Revd George Pagett, who presided over the Congregational Chapel set in Derwent Street East. Adjacent on the east side were J.T.Tomlinson & Co, builders.

Upper Bainbridge Street looking towards Ambrose Street. The bowler-hatted gentleman with the flat-topped horse-drawn delivery vehicle is loaded with small barrels and earthenware pots. The shop on the left (north) side was Mrs Ruth Riley's in 1904 but was kept for many years by Hubert Hurt. The south side shop was the grocer's belonging to Mrs Sarah Anne Bilson. The sign for William Robinson, cab proprietor, is situated at No.72.

Jerome Ltd, the photographers, began business in Derby shortly after 1935 and on 26 June 1938 they produced this view of GU 6491, the small Austin car complete with crank handle. The car is parked on Valley Road, off Warwick Avenue.

The hatted Edwardian children and dog are standing at the Mill Hill Lane intersection with Avondale Road and Swinburne Street. The three-storey, gable-fronted Victorian houses Nos.67-81 on the south side stretch right up to Renals Street where Hill View and Hill Top houses stand. George Offiler, the Derby brewer, had his residence around the corner at 11 Mill Hill Road.

Duffield Road

Close to the 'Five Lamps', the intersection of Duffield and Kedleston Road, stands the ivy-clad dentistry practice (formerly the Elms Derby Prep School). A covered wagon (probably LMS Railway) passes the chained raised causeway of Duffield Road in this 1923 view.

This second view gives a clear sight of the ornate wrought-iron lamp standard cast by Messrs Weatherhead, Glover & Co from 1839. To improve traffic flow on the Cornmarket and St Peter's Bridge area, the lamps were transferred to here in *c*.1905. The houses on Belper Road are visible in the background.

These 40 young boys on the wet playground in 1910 all belong to the Elms School for Boys situated at the junction of Duffield and Kedleston Roads (Five Lamps). The Elms was a preparatory branch of Derby School and Miss S.N.Askwith was the headmistress in charge of terms and boarding fees. An advertisement placed in the *Court Guide & County Blue Book* for 1908 tells us: 'The house is commodious and well situated, and the sanitary arrangements are perfect. There is a large garden and playground. The school cricket and football ground, gymnasium, rifle range and five tennis courts are used by the Preparatory Boys.' The building dates to *c*.1880 and was built by the Davenports.

Duffield Road appears very narrow with its cobbled edges in this 1911 view looking towards Derwent Park. The children are close to the fine balustraded house Lawnside (No.183 today) on the south side above Broadway.

This unusual comic skit relating to a darkened Penny Long Lane off Broadway was part of the 'Spoon' series of postcards published in 1909-10.

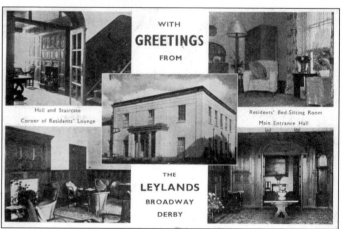

This advertisement multi-view card was published for the Linen & Woollen Drapers' Institution & Cottage Homes by the proprietors of the trade journal *Corsetry & Underwear* in 1953 and features the Leyland's on Broadway. The Queen visited the Leyland's cottage homes on 28 March 1957.

This view was No.747 in Francis William Scarratt's series of local photographic postcards during 1913, of Penny Long Lane. The notice in the middle left refers to the Leylands which was the former residence of Alderman William Leaper Newton and built in 1820. The Newtons were gone by 1921 and the drapers' retirement homes were built in the early 1950s when the Leyland house was renamed Eborn house.

Kedleston Road

Both pony and trap and early motor car wait patiently, in the sun at the West Avenue intersection with Kedleston Road. The procession coming down Kedleston Road towards Five Lamps is the occasion of Lord Curzon's visit to Derby on 28 July 1904. The ivy clad house at the intersection of Kedleston Road and Duffield Road is the Elms, which at this time was home to the surgeon William Ogle MDMA, and later became a preparatory school for Derby School.

When the Rt Hon George Nathaniel, 1st Marquis Curzon KG, become Derby's seventh Honorary Freeman of the Borough in July 1904, he was presented with this fine gilded casket and scroll. The scroll details tell us that the honour was agreed in Derby Town Hall on Wednesday, 1 June 1904.

In 1898 the Rt Hon George Curzon PC GCSI GCIE took the title Baron Curzon of Kedleston. His father, Lord Scarsdale, was lord of the manor and sole landowner. George became Earl Curzon of Kedleston in 1911 and Marquis Curzon in 1921.

William Hart, Mayor of Derby, is seated as Lord Curzon makes an address in Derby Drill Hall on 28 July 1904. The grand occasion was the presentation of the Freedom of the Borough of Derby to Lord Curzon, Viceroy of India.

The man in the white apron is Robert Irish, the butcher from the right corner with Redshaw Street. He is possibly discussing some news about the war in this 1914 view looking up Kedleston Road towards the town centre with Statham Street off to the left. The grocery premises of Howard & Co are on the right at 125 Kedleston Road.

St Aiden's was situated on the corner of Kedleston Road with Ceder Street and was known as the 'Iron Church' due to its corrugated iron fabric. Like most churches it had its own football team, St Aiden's Junior FC. The vicar, helpers and the junior XI are captured in this *c*.1910 view.

St Aiden's FC. The senior XI in *c*.1909.

A sea of children are gathered in the quadrangle of Kedleston Road Council School for the Empire Day celebrations on 24 May 1913. Alderman Brigden (a former mayor) is involved in some form of action song with the infants, several of whom have their hands raised in the air. This public elementary school originally accommodated 356 boys, 356 girls and 320 infants. At this time Arthur Hayman was the master, Miss E.Bennett the girls' mistress and Miss F.Redfern the infants' mistress. Many of the infant's mothers watch proceedings from beyond the school railings.

Patriotism was high on the agenda in this second view of Empire Day celebrations for Kedleston Road Council School in May 1913.

Long hair and pigtails are definitely the order of the day in this view showing the Standard Five class of Kedleston Road Council School during the Coronation year of 1911. Out of the 36 girls, 26 have hair ribbons, eight have flower buttonholes, only one a pair of spectacles and very few smiles.

This unusual view of Kedleston Road shows the west side between Highfield Road and White Street in c.1908. John King's (senior) nurseries stand to the right and were called Parkfields Nurseries. By 1912 Mrs J.King was looking after the nursery and florist's business where Joseph King was the nurseryman. What was to become Parkfield Cedars grammar school for girls opened in 1917 in the area between Bromley Street and Ceder Street, a little further north of here.

During the 1880s George Wheeldon, the maltster (Seven Stars Yard), lived at Parkfield House. John Moody, solicitor of the firm Moody & Wooley, lived at the adjacent Parkfield Cedars where eventually Derby's Municipal School for Girls opened on 24 April 1917.

The first secondary school for girls was Parkfield Cedars School situated near Cedar Street on Kedleston Road with Miss Margaret J.Keay as the headmistress. This c.1930s view shows the new science block with its many windows.

The oak-panelled hall of Parkfield Ceders, complete with stage and piano, looks very grand in this late 1930s view.

It is medal time during the 1925 sports day for Parkfield Cedars Secondary School for Girls.

Edward Thomas Ann (later Sir) of West Parkfield House, and Edward Hulse of Parkfield House, were long-time residents in Wheeldon Avenue off Kedleston Road. This somewhat faded view is looking towards Park Grove from Kedleston Road.

The 25-strong Kedleston Street Brass Band represented the Bourne Primitive Methodist Chapel situated on the east corner of Kedleston Street and Back Parker Street. The Bourne Primitive Methodist Sunday Schools were situated on the west corner with Parker Street. The chapel was erected in 1870, being an edifice of brick and stone costing £5,500 and providing seating for 900. The bandmaster in this view was Mr T.A.Bailey, who was a draper at 118 Abbey Street. The secretary was Frederick William Lewis, a shopkeeper of 70 Whitecross Street and Bradley Street.

C.W.Lee took this view of White Street in 1909.

St Anne's Church, situated in Whitecross Street, was erected in 1871-72 at a cost of £4,000. There were 12 stained-glass windows, six of which were presented by W.H.Worthington Esq in 1875, and three by Mrs Worthington in 1894 in memory of her husband. As can be seen in this 1912 interior view, the walls of the east end and sanctuary were decorated with paintings representing 'Events in the Life of Our Lord'. There was originally room for 600 worshippers here.

The highly ornate font of St Anne's has been decorated with both fresh flowers and potted flowering plants in this c.1910 scene.

This charming scene depicts the Brook Street Pleasant Sunday Afternoon outing in c.1903. They were probably associated with the United Methodist Free Church on the north side of Brook Street in Derby's West End. Only two violins and two brass wind instruments but presumably several good voices! Their packed lunch appears to be in the parcel on the grass.

George Wallis, shopkeeper of 135 Watson Street, sold this view of Moore, Eady & Murcott Goode Ltd's factory on Markeaton Street (off Mackworth Road) from his retail premises. They were hosiery manufacturers and the site previously belonged to the paint manufacturing mills of Ellam, Jones & Co Ltd.

Characters in the making seems to fit the bill for these five West End kids. This late Edwardian photograph taken somewhere in Derby's notorious West End shows how tough life could be for some. The tall boy on the left has a black eye patch and no shoes! The house behind with the dubious drapes had no carpets on the floor.

London Road

There were no motor ambulances at the time of this 1905 view of the Derbyshire Royal Infirmary. The DRI was rebuilt in 1891 and Queen Victoria laid the foundation stone on 21 May that year.

This later view, taken during the 1930s, shows that the DRI was built on the pavilion principle with connecting glass corridor. The tennis courts lie to the left and right of the main block.

Gypsies, Pixie and Charlie's Aunt were all part of the fund raising activities in aid of the Derbyshire Royal Infirmary in the early 1920s. The placard held by Charlie's Aunt reads: 'Charlie's Aunt going to Wembley?', a possible reference to Derby County's hope of beating West Ham in the 1923 FA Cup semi-final. The very first Hospital Day Carnival was 4 September 1920 and the procession from the town centre would wind their way to Markeaton Park, where these two views were taken.

The matron and nurses are flanked by ornate Victorian garden urns at the entrance to the Royal Derbyshire Nursing Institute in 1904. The institute was originally under the patronage of Queen Victoria and founded in 1895. At that time it was listed as the Royal Derby & Derbyshire Nursing Sanitary Association. The objects of the institution were 'to provide thoroughly trained nurses among the poor and in private families and to organise means that would tend to prevention and more or less directly to the removal of disease'. The first lady super-intendent was Mrs Woodhead before Miss Agnes Atthill took over the reigns for many years.

The Nightingale Home at 1 Trinity Street was associated with the Royal Derby and Derbyshire Nursing Institution, and from the beginning Miss Agnes Atthill was also the lady superintendent here. This nursing home was also a training school for midwives and district nurses. This late afternoon view was taken in 1913.

The unveiling of the Florence Nightingale statue by the Duke of Devonshire at the Derbyshire Royal Informary on 12 June 1914. The Mayor, Samuel Johnson, and the Mayoress stand to the right of the duke on the makeshift wooden platform. Florence Nightingale's father designed their first home at Lea Hurst near Matlock, but she spent little time there. After the Crimean War she returned there for a spell but died at her London home on 13 August 1910 at the age of 90.

Taken shortly after the unveiling ceremony in 1914, this photograph shows the fine work of the sculptress, Countess Greichen.

H.E.Pearse of London Road was the photographer who took this fine study of an unknown nurse with St John armband working at the Derbyshire Royal Infirmary in c.1912.

Frederick J.Boyes was the photographer responsible for this July 1917 photograph of young nurse, 'Kathleen from the DRI'.

This being the DRI's 99th anniversary parade positively dates the photograph to June 1909 as the original DRI, designed by William Strutt, opened on 4 June 1810. The message written on the reverse side reads: 'This is not the King's Own going to the church, but the Mayor's Own coming from church. We had some fine singing.' This view is from Irongate looking to the corner of St Mary's Gate and Queen Street. The premises of William Scott, clothier, and Clarke & Winfield, milliners, are clearly visible.

Messrs W.W.Winter were the producers of this picture postcard in 1915, for sale at 2d each to raise funds for the war wounded in the DRI. J.H.Byard was a prolific local still-life painter producing many oil paintings well into the late 1930s. He lived at 20 North Avenue, Mickleover, close to the famous photographer F.W. Scarratt.

Thirteen nurses to 18 wounded does not seem a bad ratio in this late 1915 wartime view inside the King's Ward at the DRI.

There was definitely no shortage of help in this *c.*1920 view of the DRI's Out patients' treatment room as four nurses and six doctors deal with the day's intake of injured. Note the two wooden tressels in use to enable foot and leg injuries to be treated. The doctor standing to the right of the rear screen with bow tie appears to be wearing black rubber gloves, or is it a false hand? Nurse Rawlings can be seen on the left of the screen.

Five stalwarts of the Derbyshire Royal Infirmary staff pose for the photographer in this turn of the century insight into life in the kitchens. There must be hundreds of tiles here, together with modern electric lighting.

Electric Tram Car No.27 has just passed Samuel Whybrow's restaurant and dining rooms and approaches the Station Inn on the north side of Midland Road in early 1906. The large premises on the corner of London Road on the south side belong to Frederick Dalton, the gramophone dealer. The famous Alexander Rooms on the top floor of Derby photographers W.W.Winter are next after Sidney Woodward's hairdresser's shop.

'We always have a Worthington at Alf Leigh's.' was the advertisement put out by the Station Inn on Midland Road. Alf Leigh, complete with fob chain, forms part of Leigh's football and cricket XI who represented the Station Inn c.1914. Worthington, along with Bass from the jug, is the present day fall-down potion delivered by landlord David J.Lalor, and pool and martial arts are his forté. The Station Inn has recently undergone sympathetic alterations.

This 'ASRS' card depicts the discharged MR Goods Guards, Derby, who lost their jobs as a result of taking part in the 1911 Railway Strike. The card was sold for their benefit. Back row (left to right): W.Jenkinson (14 years' service), D.Cadman (17 years), J.Ewins (11 years). Front row: J.Cutts (11 years), W.J.Short (20 years), G.H.Dalley (14 years).

Please buy a Post-Card—1d. each—and help to support **1865** Orphan Children of the A.S.R.S. And for each Post-Card you have a chance to win the Train, the same being made and given by Bro. W. Thrupp, 126, Holcombe Street, Derby. Post-Cards can be had from the above address. The Train is 8 feet 7 inches long, and the weight is 32 lbs. The winning number will be published in the "Derby Daily Telegraph" and "Railway Review," December 21st, 1906.

Brother W.Thrupp was very active in supporting the Associated Society of Railway Servants (ASRS) and this and the previous fund-raising postcard were available from him at 126 Holcombe Street off Dairy House Road for 1d each. William Thrupp was recorded as a shopkeeper at 215 Harrington Street, at the corner of Holcombe Street, by 1912.

This train was made by Brother W.Thrupp and the number of this card (11,834) was entered into a prize draw to help support the 1,865 orphaned children of ASRS. The train was 8ft 7ins long and weighed 32lbs. The winning number was published in the *Derby Evening Telegraph* and *Railway Review* on 21 December 1906.

C.S.Swift from the Midland Art Studio at 125 Normanton Road produced this view of the banner belonging to the National Union of Railway Men (NUR) of Derby & District. The banner promotes the NUR's beliefs of 'Safety, Repairs, All Men are Brethren, Brothers in Conference and God Bless our orphans.' This 1920s view is believed to be inside the NUR's base at Unity Hall situated where Normanton and Burton Roads meet at the end of Green Lane.

Electric tram car No.23 waits to depart from the Midland Station to the Peartree terminus in *c.*1905. On the left the ornate tower of the Midland Railway Institute on Railway Terrace is visible.

The YMCA hut, pictured here, was provided for the benefit of travelling soldiers and was erected on 21 April 1917. It was later removed to Mickleover and in 1998 still serves as a branch library in Station Road.

Jig and toolmaking was a respected and skilled profession for these three cloth-capped workers in one of the Derby Loco Works shops in *c.*1913.

The 31-strong Midland Railway Service Messroom Band, complete with seven trilbies, 22 flat caps and two without any headgear, pose for this Christmas 1921 study. Four trombones, four tubas, ten coronets and eight trumpets make up the band.

Mr J.B.Lloyd was the proprietor of the Victoria Inn at 12 Midland Place, opposite the Railway Institute, during the early 1930s. At that time the Victoria Inn was one of the few Derby pubs to admit children. It was advertised as being 'half a minute to the right of the Midland Station, possessing a splendid conservatory' and sold Eadie's fine ales. This view of the conservatory shows that Mr Lloyd was a keen horticulturist with the hanging baskets and many other plants. The inn dates to c.1860 and was owned by James Eadie Ltd until Bass Brewery took it over by 1937.

Jedbury Junior was the title of the drama performed by the Midland Institute Dramatic Society in this early 1905 publication by Charles H.Foster of St James's Street.

This postcard was sent to Miss Proctor at 7 Upper Madeley Street to remind her of the resumption of Mr T.W.Cowlinshaw's shorthand evening classes at the Midland Railway Institute in January 1905.

MISS REMINGTON'S REVERIE.

42, Wilfred St.,

DERBY. *Jany. 7/05* -

The Shorthand Classes at the Midland Railway Institute resume on Wednesday *Jany II*. when the Instructor Mr. T.W. Cowlishaw will be pleased to welcome old students and any others they may be able to induce to join.
Speed .. .. 6.45 to 8.0 pm
Elementary &
Intermediate 8. 0 to 9.0 pm.

Fee 3/6 per quarter.

Twenty-seven miniature portraits of the leading Midland Railway Company dignitaries together with their facsimile signatures form the basis of this 1877 production.

The Railway Institute, standing on the corner of Midland Place and Railway Terrace, was designed by the Midland Railway's own architect, Charles Trubshaw. Railway employees could gain membership by having a small contribution deducted from their pay. The institute contained a lecture and concert room, games rooms, dining room and restaurant, and a prestigious library with over 16,000 volumes . The splendid facilities were a generous gift by the proprietors of the railway company to employees of all grades. The 27 ladies, one youth and one pet cat pictured here were the original staff when it opened in 1892 on the site occupied by many former North Midland Railway houses. Nearly all the staff are wearing a flower arrangement to adorn their smart but sombre black Victorian garments.

A lot of changes have taken place since this 1968 view of Derby 4 shed was taken. St Andrew's Church was demolished in 1970. The St Andrew's goods depot has been flattened to facilitate extensive car parking for the Railway Contractor Offices at Nelson Street, housing Midland Main Line, Balfour Beatty Rail Maintenance etc. To the left there are still signs of the turntable removal following a tank engine derailment.

This sketch is an extract from an early Victorian scrapbook belonging to Edward Bradbury ('Strephon'), the Derby author. This interesting piece is a hand-drawn pencil sketch of the site of the Midland Station, Derby, dated 1836, exactly four years before the Francis Thompson-designed station was opened. This sketch is believed to be the only one in existence and hence it is of great importance in terms of understanding the area the station was to be built on. A small cottage and many trees were soon to disappear with the coming of the railway.

R.K.Peacock produced this late Victorian cabinet photograph from his 'Spot' studio on St Peter's Street, Derby, of an unknown Midland Railway servant.

Electric tram car No.14 is just passing Traffic Street on the left on its way to the Midland Station where Frank Porter has his furniture removal business at 88 Traffic Street. The first premises after Traffic Street are the Telegraph Inn followed by John Sexton's tobacconist's and then the Prince of Wales beer retail outlet also owned by Sexton.

The small friendly Priory Commercial Hotel was situated at 111 London Road, Derby, and in 1912 was run by Mrs Nellie Tooley; by 1928 Bernard W. Tooley was in charge. This view shows the fine dining room, hotel front and a bedroom complete with brass bed and washstand with jug and bowl *c.*1914.

The superb coach work of Thomas Lloyd & Co's motor hearse is apparent in this *c.*1912 view. Lloyd's funeral carriage and motor hearse business was located at 35 London Road. He also advertised the best makes in ladies' and gents' calf and kid gloves.

This early photograph was posted to a Miss M. Marsh in Barbados, in the West Indies, on 25 August 1904 and arrived there on 12 September. Both horse-drawn delivery vehicle and horse-tram are opposite the London Road Wesleyan Chapel on the corner of Canal Street. This chapel was erected in 1861 and consisted of a gabled front, flanked by two turrets surmounted by short spires and had a

sitting for 850 of which 250 were free. The trees have grown considerably in the last 94 years, and in 1964 the chapel received a modern curved brick frontage.

Left: W. W. Winter took this midday view of Holy Trinity Church in London Road in *c.*1906. A blind beggar can just be seen leaning against the garden wall of the parsonage (could this be the famous John Darwin? Winter's won much acclaim for their sympathetic portraiture of him). The church register dates to 1837 but the church was completely rebuilt in 1904 when the former St George's dedication was dropped in favour of Holy Trinity. The Revd Walter Waddelow Martin MA was the vicar here from 1902.

Locals enjoy the sun-drenched paved area leading to Castlefields Main Centre shopping precinct. ASA Discounts with the Eastern Carpet Stores beneath dominate the square. Many changes have taken place since Scarratt & Co Ltd published this 1963 view.

The Oldershaws were a prolific Derby butcher's family from the early 1920s through to modern times. Alfred, Alfred Borrey and Frank had premises in Clifford Street Osmaston, and No.5 and No.33 the Market Hall respectively. Alfred Borrey Oldershaw and his daughter are pictured at the entrance to their shop at 653 London Road on the corner of Warwick Street in the mid-1920s. The shop eventually became Oldershaw & Sons and Francis Oldershaw maintained a family presence at No.9 the Market Hall.

Electric tram No.24 is opposite the opening to Borough's Walk on the right where John Hargreaves Temperance Hotel stands on the corner with Ward & Co, the tailors. The stately Congregational Church with its entrance beneath a fine portico, supported by Corinthian pillars, dominates the east side of London Road adjacent to the old Traffic Street. It was originally built by Derby architect Henry I.Stevens in April 1843 and opened as the Coliseum cinema in 1934 before demolition in 1962 as part of the further widening of Traffic Street.

Several hundred people including many children are lined up on London Road outside the old Congregational Chapel in readiness for their majesties the King and Queen passing through on their way to the Royal Show on 5 July 1933, shortly before the chapel was converted to a cinema. The long ladder to the front was allegedly left there by the builders W.Ford & Sons for nearly two years while a legal dispute took place over whether a church should be converted into a place of entertainment.

The Liversage's Almshouses were erected in 1863 out of the Liversage estate at a cost of £3,000 and consisted of 13 brick houses. The charity, left by Robert Liversage in the year 1529, was at the time of small value, but by 1888 amounted to £2,600 pounds yearly consisting of land and house property in and near Derby. The houses would originally have housed 70 old men and women who were selected (when vacancies occurred through death) from the parish of St Peter's only by the vicar and church wardens. A chapel and concert room were built at the rear and friends frequently provided concerts and varied entertainment for the amusement and recreation of the old people. Robert Liversage was a wealthy tradesman who lived in the parish of St Peter's in the reign of Henry VIII. This view was taken in c.1914.

This later view depicts the almshouses decorated with bunting in readiness for the royal visit of King George V and Queen Mary in July 1933. The plane tree close to the bench is already 64 years old and was one of many instituted by Jon Davis in 1869.

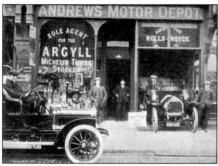

A.Andrews established his motor depot on the west side of London Road in *c.*1905, shortly after leaving his motor mills in Coventry. This 1906 view shows the forecourt of his motor depot and show-room containing CH A2. They were the sole agents for Crossley, Belsize and Talbot cars. Mr Andrews can be seen in the doorway, complete with bowler hat.

CH 363 and other prestigious 'new fangled' motor cars are parked at the workshops and garages to the rear of Andrews' motor depot. Both open and closed cars were for hire and the business was open day and night.

Richard Keene, the notable Derby photographer, took this view of St Andrew's Middle Class School on London Road adjacent to St Andrew's Church during the late 1870s. The school was erected in 1869 for 150 children. At the time of this view Mr George Sutherland was the headmaster, as he had been since its foundation, and Thomas Clarke Story the second master. Mr Sutherland and masters are gathered in the rear playground.

George Sutherland, the headmaster (bearded centre), is again captured by Richard Keene with his other masters and clergy in *c.*1878 on the steps leading to his school. The school was founded in 1869 by Revd Canon J.Erskine, then vicar of St Andrew's. The aim of the founder 'was to place within the means of the middle classes and tradesmen of the town, a school where the fees were moderate and the instruction sound'.

William Gillan, one of Derby's first photographers, situated in Oaks Yard off St Peter's Street, took this early 1880s picture of George Sutherland's son.

These two photographs were the 'rough proofs' produced by W.W. Winter on Midland Road and show George Sutherland and his daughter in the early 1870s.

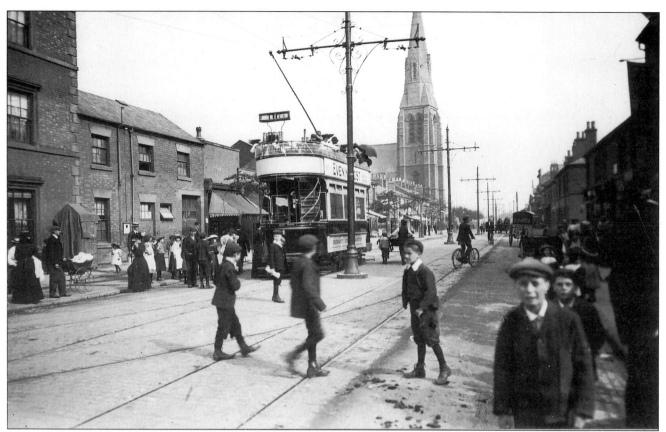

A sizeable queue, mainly children, waits on the east side of London Road ready to board open-top tram No.4 bound for Alvaston on 28 July 1904, the day after the opening day of Derby's electric trams. At least 20 different shops and business existed at this time along the east side from Midland Road to Hulland Street, including saddler's William Webb.

The open-top electric tram car No.44 has just passed Barlow Street on the left of this *c.*1911 view published by Alfred Goodere, newsagent of Nightingale Road. The tram lines in the left foreground are those from Bateman Street. St Andrew's School and Church are to the right after the L & NW Railway hoarding. St Andrew's was essentially a 'railway church'. The expansion of the railways and its employees necessitated it and the Midland Railway contributed greatly to the building fund.

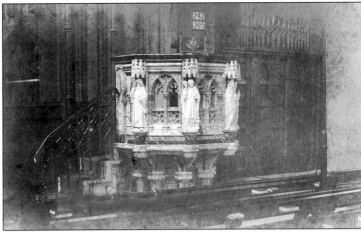

The Lever Brothers of Derby published this unusual photograph depicting the decorative pulpit inside St Andrew's Church in c.1907. The vicar at the time was Revd Richard Arthur Hay, who was the incumbent from 1901-12. The church was chiefly erected in 1866, from designs by Sir George Gilbert Scott RA, and seated 800.

Bemrose & Sons of Derby printed the church monthly for St Andrew's, which sold for 1d. This issue is No.26 from February 1898 and tells us that St Andrew's churchwardens were congratulated for collecting the largest sum ever raised in one year.

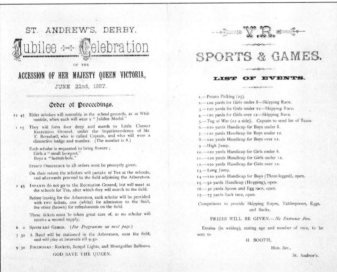

The celebrations for Queen Victoria's Jubilee held on 22 June 1887 gives us an insight into the strictness of obedience and the great attention to detail of the schools' regime in Victorian times. In addition to the middle class boy's school there were also boys', girls' and infants' schools under competent tuition, four Bible classes on Sunday, a reading room and a library, Mothers' Union meetings and a clothing club. Hence it was a very comprehensive and compact set of parochial buildings where a large church, four schools, offices and a vicarage all existed in one enclosure as the previous picture shows.

The shadows of the soldiers presenting arms are displayed on the flagstones inside the gated archway leading to St Andrew's Church, schools and vicarage. Sherwood Foresters are on the march up London Road. The advertising hoardings were on this site for many years and help us to date this view as 1914, as the *Yorkshire Post* advertises: 'The first and fullest war news.' Other advertisements included the Cosy Cinema (opened 1913), Grand Theatre and Agricultural Show.

The spire of St Andrew's Church is visible in the distant right as the 70-strong party of Sherwood Foresters march up London Road. The ornate gateway on the right led to the LNW and North Staffs Railway Co's Goods Yard and Cattle Station. Opposite on the west side of London Road (116) stands the premises of Gentles & King. Robert William Gentles was an eminent physician and surgeon while Thomas Laurie Gentles was a medical officer and public vaccinator for Derby South district. The building later became a Temperance Hotel and eventually the Carlton Hotel.

Henry Boden, the Temperance campaigner and lace manufacturer whose residence was The Friary, had these almshouses built in 1891 to designs by the Methodist architect John Wills for his firm's pensioners. The central portion housed the inter-denominational chapel and this photograph records the site on Castle Street close to his manufactory on London Street (Castlefields) in 1909. They were demolished in 1957 to pave the way for the Main Centre shopping development.

Over 30 Derby youngsters brave the elements and only one does not take up the expected cover-up stance. Penned on the reverse side is 'Open air pool, Siddals Road'. However this is unlikely to be one of the two pools built by Michael Thomas Bass in 1873 and is more likely to be Markeaton Recreation Ground.

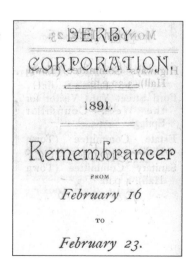

Left: This fine portrait of Ruth Selvey, who ran a shop in the Siddals Road area, was taken by Frederick J. Boyes of Derby. She was the grandmother to one of the daring boys, Master A.H.Selvey, in the open-air pool previously shown. In the late 1890s Ruth was a fishmonger at 12 Willow Row, a business which was taken over by Reuben Hurd some little time after 1900.

Right: During the 1890s, Derby Corporation produced many 'remembrances' for their committee members. This particular one for 1891 refers to the Bass's Recreation Ground. Baths visitor for 16 February is shown as Councillor Ellis, while Councillor Spriggs was down for visiting Ford Street Yard. Dates for Sanitary, Parliamentary, Markets committee meetings etc., were also included.

The houses of Litchurch Street have long since disappeared but hopefully little Reggie and Kenneth, pictured here outside their house in the 1940s, have survived.

A huge crowd (predominantly women) has gathered to watch the local dignitaries and 20 or so choir boys perched precariously on the scaffolding of the stone-laying ceremony of the new St Osmund's Church, whose register dates from 1743, during August 1904. The timber scaffolding was lashed together with rope.

This somewhat isolated view was taken approximately seven years after St Osmund's opened in 1905. The church was situated on London Road, cost £5,940 to build and was constituted the parish church of Osmaston (near Derby). It originally had seating for 540. The Revd Lancelot Sydney Currey MA was the vicar at this time.

The Crompton & Evans Bank (later NatWest) is not yet built on the corner with Midland Road in this c.1911 view. The site is still occupied by Henry Hodgkinson, the pork butcher and noted polony and brawn maker. On the opposite corner of Regent Street the grocery business of Alfred Butterworth exists.

Councillor and Mrs Boam, the Mayor and Mayoress of Derby, sent this gold-embossed Christmas card to their friends and colleagues in 1895. The Borough crest adorns the front while their address at Litchurch Villa is inside.

A 1920s aerial view of George Fletcher & Co's Derby works situated off Litchurch Lane. Both the company's malleable foundries and sugar machinery works were here. Osmaston Road is in the foreground as it crosses the main railway line.

A party of foreign engineers on a fact-finding mission to George Fletcher's foundry during the late 1940s. Most keep their distance from the extreme heat as molten iron is poured under the control of a foundry worker perched precariously on top of a sloping wheel barrow.

The complexity of the machinery is evident in this postwar view inside the machine shop of George Fletcher & Co. The advertisement plaque on the floor bears the date 12 April 1947. This is their Masson Works on Litchurch Lane where they manufactured items for the chemical and engineering industry together with sugar manufacturing equipment.

Mansfield Road

Frederick Gaves, landlord of the Bridge Inn on Mansfield Road, has joined his family at the deck chairs enjoying the sun close to the landing stage on the River Derwent in 1909. Boats could be hired on the Bridge Inn dock. A Derby Regatta poster adorns the building where the boats were stored out of season. The Bridge Inn was established in c.1850, in a large former private home dating from the 1790s.

Some members of the Gaves family have taken to the water for this second view on what was obviously a very fine day in 1909. The public house was named after the nearby St Mary's Bridge, and underwent major internal reconstruction in 1989. Local man Roy Salt can remember catching crayfish near the weir in 1933.

George Groome's decorative public house, the Coach & Horses, stands on the corner of Mansfield Road and Old Chester Road where Charrington's Ales were served. The marquee erected to the left in the garden is in readiness for some unknown function in 1908. This view is looking from Mansfield Road (A608) looking directly at the neat terraced row of Old Chester Road leading down to the River Derwent.

These terraced houses on Chester Green Road are much the same today. The ornate gas lamp standard confirms that we are at the junction with Mansfield Road as the name is etched into the glass. The two council workers appear to be drawing water from the mains hydrant to fill their horse-drawn water cart. The reflection in the window of J. Vince's general store clearly shows the presence of an old chimney stack.

All smiles for the photographer (C.W.Lee) from these six Edwardian youngsters in the middle of Chester Green Road. This view is looking towards Mansfield Road from the corner of Marcus Street in 1908.

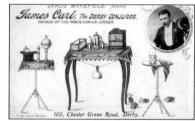

James Wakefield (formerly known as James Carl) was a well-known Derby conjurer who resided at 100 Chester Green Road. He was a painter and decorator by trade and his 'magic circle' work was only part-time. This card was distributed to advertise his services for birthday parties, weddings, dinners and all manner of social occasions.

Mrs Mary A.Burman, the shopkeeper of 194 Mansfield Road, stands outside her mainly confectionery shop on the corner with Roman Road. Several other people are also obviously aware that the photographer is about. This 1908 view is taken from Mansfield Road looking down Roman Road towards Stores Road.

This later 1930s card shows James now has white hair and spectacles and has been performing to children for 25 years. A member of the Inner Magic Circle, London. James would apparently deliver original and strictly refined performances that left audiences talking of his performances for months afterwards.

The semaphore railway bracket signal is just visible in this 1911 view looking down New Chester Street towards St Mary's Goods Yard and the main railway line. Many of the local residents, including the landlord and landlady of the City Tavern, have turned out for photographer C.W.Lee.

The intersection of Mansfield Road (A608) and Alfreton Road (A61) looks deserted in this 1940s view taken from the opening to Old Chester Road. The iron bridge of the Friargate line spans the Alfreton Road. The road sign denotes 22 miles to Mansfield and 9 miles to Ripley (seems low). The old Parker Foundry stands on the left of the A608 with its landmark chimney.

Normanton Road

This faded view of *c.*1910 is of Bestria Villa in Belgrave Street which runs from Salisbury Street to Normanton Road. The unknown family commissioned this view in order to send it to, among other people, friends in Wirksworth.

The highly-regarded Burton upon Trent photographer J.S.Simnett produced this *c.*1905 view of where Green Lane meets Babington Lane, at the junction with Normanton Road. The open-top tram is close to Jonathan Staley's Babington Arms Inn which sold Stretton's Derby Ales. C.A.Grimley's draper's shop was on the right corner with Babington Lane for several years.

Francis William Scarratt, the 'people's photographer, took this photograph of the Alexandra Skating Rink at 115 Normanton Road in *c.*1911, two years after it opened. The former ice skating rink at this time was a roller skating rink and 13 youngsters are awaiting to gain entrance. Derby architect Thomas Harrison Thorpe of 23 St James's Street converted the Alexandra into a cinema during October 1913. It closed in May 1953. The Trocadero Ballroom sprang up on this site under the proprietorship of Sammy Ramsden but burnt down in October 1982. Flats now occupy the site which is known as Trocadero Court.

The Alexandra Roller Skating Rank was on the corner with Hartington Street and Normanton Road and opened on Saturday, 15 May 1909 at 2.30pm. This artistic 'glamour' card, produced by the notable publishers David Allen & Sons Ltd, was in fact an entrance ticket to the opening of the rink by the Mayor of Derby, Alderman Sir Henry Howe Bemrose. The manager at this time was Mr W.H.Innes.

A interior view tells us that only two of the male participants are equipped for roller skating. The blunt signs at the rear of the rink read: 'Gentlemen. Please skate with hats removed', 'Please watch this sign — Clear the floor — No fast skating allowed.' A small brass band is seated in readiness for the opening night in 1909. The remainder are all staff associated with running the Alexandra.

This second view shows the well-stocked Normanton Road window of Proctor & Co in the parish of Litchurch. All manner of clothes could be purchased here — cloth caps, overcoats, jackets etc — and Proctor's were renowned for their good value. Items in this window vary from 1s 11d to 25s. Mr Proctor (with the beard) and his assistant are pictured here in 1910 when the shop window still contains an old gas mantle lamp.

This view shows, Proctor & Co's clothing store on the corner with Grove Street and the window display strangely contains no clothes, only advertisements and designs. The poster to the left (almost out of view) advertises the Alexandra Skating Rink being open every Monday, Wednesday and Saturday with admission prices of 3d and 6d. By 1928, through to at least the late 1930s, the shop was run by Miss Gertrude.

Another view from Charles William Lee of Abbey Street. He photographed Grove Street in 1908 looking towards Osmaston Road from the Normanton Road end. On the right-hand, south side the corner shop of Ernest Milward, beer retailer, is visible on the corner with Twyford Street. Just beyond here lies the entrance to the tree-lined Arboretum and the Arboretum Lodge. Both the south and north sides of the street are littered with advertising hoardings.

About The Rams

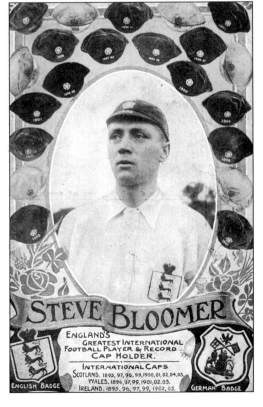

As an England player, Derby County's Steve Bloomer scored 28 goals in 21 appearances which remained a record until 1956. His first cap was won in 1895. He is still the Rams' record scorer with 332 League and FA Cup goals. This card was produced in the 1930s by Wainwright's (later Carter's), the Derby printers.

Steve Bloomer was signed by Derby County after promising performances in the Derbyshire Minor League where he once scored 14 goals in one game. This artist's impression of the immortal Bloomer was used as an advertisement for the *Umpire* Sunday newspaper in 1903.

Derby County football team of 1889-90, their second season in the Football League which was formed in April 1888. Back row (left to right): W.Chatterton, A.Williamson, A.Latham, A. Goodall, H.Dakin (trainer), A.Ferguson, W.Roulstone, J.Bulmer (umpire). Front row: G. Bakewell, A.Higgins, J.Goodall, S.Holmes, L.Cooper, R.Milarvie.

In 1914, Steve Bloomer was coaching in Germany when war broke out and he was interned at Ruhleben and, together with Blackburn's Sam Wolstenholme, a fellow England international, he ran a football league in the camp throughout the war. This photograph records the teams for Bloomer's farewell match on 20 March 1918. After the war he returned to play with and coach Derby's reserve team. Bloomer is standing, seventh left, middle row.

'No Bloomer' was a comic production perhaps referring to his internment in Germany rather than the period when he left Derby to play for Middlesbrough in 1906 but returning to a huge welcome in 1910 after a transfer costing £100 at the age of 36. Steve Bloomer died in April 1938, aged 64, after a period of failing health.

The Derby Ram in comical format formed part of Ogden's *AFC Nicknames* series of 50 cigarette cards.

Derby County were in Division One during 1937-38 and this photograph was published as a postcard in Stockholm. Back row (left to right): E.Udall, L.Bailey, J.Kirby, J.W.Barker, K.Scattergood, D.Bell, H.Travis, W.Bromage (trainer). Middle row: R.Stockill, S.Wilemen, R.W.Dix, D.J.Astley, C.Napier, J.Nicholas, E.Keen, J.Howe. Front row: R.Hann, J.Hagan, F.S.Jessop, A.Jefferies, S.Crooks, D.Duncan, G.Hannah. Only three were to play in the FA Cup Final in 1946 — Jack Nicholas, Jack Howe and Dally Duncan.

Derby County's line up for the 1946 FA Cup semi-final at Hillsborough where they drew with Birmingham City before winning the replay at Maine Road. Back row (left to right): Reg Harrison, Jack Parr, Vic Woodley, Jim Bullions, Leon Leuty, Jack Stamps. Front row: Chick Musson, Raich Carter, Jack Nicholas, Peter Doherty and Dally Duncan. Jack Parr missed the Final after breaking an arm.

Jack Howe shoulders Jack Nicholas around the Wembley pitch after the Rams' 4-1 extra-time victory over Charlton Athletic in the 1946 FA Cup Final. Pin-stripe suited manager Stuart McMillan looks on with pride, while former player and assistant trainer at this time, Jack Bowers, carries the ball. This is the only time the Rams have won the FA Cup.

Dally Duncan wonders whether this Derby shot has beaten Charlton's Sam Bartram.

The Wembley crowd, together with Derby's Peter Doherty, anxiously wait to see how Sam Bartram deals with punching the ball away.

The triumphant Rams team greet the huge crowd outside Burton's the tailors on the corner of Victoria Street and St Peter's Street. The FA Cup is safe with captain Jack Nicholas. Derby's trainer Dave Willis, and players Reg Harrison, Dally Duncan, Jim Bullions, Peter Doherty and Raich Carter all look relaxed.

Offiler's beer dray sports the 'Bravo Boys' placard on its journey from the Blue Peter to Full Street Police Station (the Council House was not yet completed). Thousands turned out to see the triumphant team.

Former Rams player Arthur Latham, who resided at 7 Peach Street near Slack Lane and was recorded in 1908 as a painter, through to 1912. But he was creative in other ways as Derby County's trainer from 1891 and also trainer to the England team on occasions. He left the club some time after 1913 and was later trainer to Norwich City. Obviously a trainer's wages needed to be supplemented during this period.

Photograph of the winners of the 1945-46 six-a-side competition for the Worth Cup! Three of these players have signed the reverse side of the print: Ron Sturgess, P.Hand and L.B.Brown.

During the 1940s, Chelsea were renowned for their graphic programme covers. This publication marked the Rams' visit to Stamford Bridge on 5 April 1947 and has an obvious Easter theme. Derby lost 3-0 in front of 52,886 spectators, during a season when the Rams finished fourth in Division One.

How many of these young hopefuls made the grade? Ten players and two goalkeepers make up this happy group of the Derby Boys football team of 1956-57. Ken Blood (second right in the second row from the back) and Mr Insley (second left in the second row from the front) were sports teacher and headmaster respectively when the author attended Roe Farm Junior School in the late 1950s.

Derbyshire County Cricket Club, with only three players out of the 11 not sporting moustaches. Back row (left to right): J.Humphries, A.Warren, W.Bestwick, G.Curgenven, L.G.Wright, S.Needham. Front row: W.Storer, C.A.Ollivierre, S.M.Ashcroft (captain), S.Cadman, H.F.Wright. Charles Ollivierre was Derbyshire's first West Indian player, in 1900.

Nottingham Road

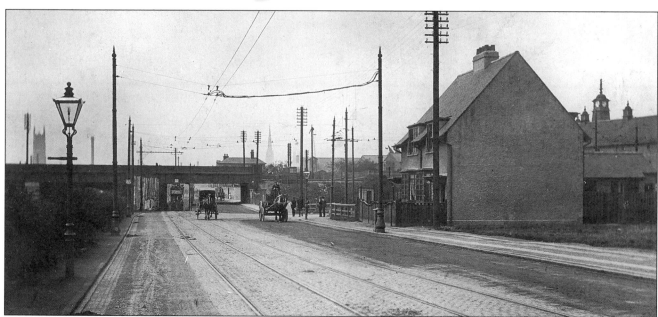

The horse and cart has just passed the old Stores Road entrance to Aiton & Co's works off Nottingham Road. In this view looking towards All Saints' and St Alkmund's in *c*.1913, Nottingham Road still has gas lamps. The railway bridge leading to Nottingham Road Station, complete with its notorious dip in the road (to accommodate tram wires), is in clear view.

Gadsby & Co were monumentalists of some repute and their monumental mason's premises were at 275 Nottingham Road on the corner with Cowsley Road. Gadsby & Co, according to their advertisements, were established in 1881 and their business was handily placed with Nottingham Road cemetery being just up the road. The old electric tram car post on the corner helps to date this view as *c*.1908. Just a few years prior to this, Ernest F. Tinkler was the monumental mason here for several years, while Gadsby's were then situated close to the Co-op coal wharves near the Derwent Street end of Nottingham Road.

George Wood, grocer and provisions merchant, had his cash store on the Nottingham Road corner with Alice Street. Two burly policemen complete with capes fastened across their shoulders await with others the royal visitors of 1906. The large 'Co-operator's' sign to the right led to the Derby Co-operative Provident Society's Limited's coal wharves.

Derwent Junior School, situated between St Mark's Road and Beaufort Street close to Nottingham Road, was certainly a very large school. The original Derwent School opened in 1932. The paddocked area in the foreground disappeared some time after this c.1950s view.

Osmaston Road

Pollard Graham & Co, photographers of Rodney Chambers, Cornmarket, took this portrait of a prize-winning beast at the 1911 Derby Cattle Show. This beast was sold to Frederick Wright, the butcher on the corner of Sacheveral Street and Osmaston Road. The message on the reverse side, addressed to C.E.Taylor, butcher, Bank Row, Matlock, reads: 'Dear Sir, we have no hind quarters of mutton to spare this week, as we have eight or ten forequarters hanging now.'

William Alton, building contractor of Osmaston Road, prefabricated this lorry show float to advertise his building products at the Derby Show during the 1930s. His mottos were: 'Alton Built means Better Built' and 'Busy as a Bee Builder'.

The Metalite Ltd Works were situated on Gresham Road off Osmaston Road. They were manufacturers of incandescent electric lamps. David S.Butler, the London Road stationers, produced this c.1913 view of a lady and her seven children outside the works when they appear to be closed, possibly on a Sunday. The building had a variety of uses, producing mica, wallpaper and braidings over several years. To the left down Hawthorn Street was where the World War Two canteen stood.

The Metalite Works of Gresham Road in the previous view were formally occupied by Henry Hill & Co Ltd, the incandescent mantle manufacturers, for a few years only c.1906-08. This view shows the manager and manageress in the laboratory mixing the acids for the mantles.

Twelve ladies are working in Henry Hill & Co's Impregnating & Drying Room. The interesting message from 'Mabel' on the reverse side and posted in July 1908 reads: 'Dear Cecil, I am coming round to see you now [32 Sale Street] as I shall have more time as they kicked us all out. No more work so we have got to walk the streets now. The place has gone smash, 250 of us out of work. Pip pip, old dear.'

Charles McCann's well-known musical instrument emporium was titled as McCann's Piano and Organ Saloon and situated at 15-17 Osmaston Road.

The Derby Pierrots have attracted a substantial audience on a warm summer's day in Darley Abbey Park on the Derby Lifeboat Demonstration Day of 17 July 1909. Five of the troupe sit this one out while one of the pierrots performs a solo with piano accompaniment on Platform 1. Derby's Mayor of 1909, William Blews Robotham, a former solicitor and Temperance preacher, organised this lifeboat gala to raise funds for the National Lifeboat Institution.

Sergeant J.H.Booth of Lady Grove Cottages, Osmaston Road, was secretary of the Derbyshire Imperial Veterans' Association. This view shows Mrs Walter Salmond of Newton Old Hall, Alfreton with six of the veterans. Mr Booth and Mrs Salmond both invited applications for their veterans as follows: 'Members of above may be engaged to act as doorkeepers or any other post at bazaars, or other public functions on application to the Secretary.'

Several Edwardian children pose for the photographer close to the main entrance to Derby Royal Agricultural Society's Show in 1906 on Osmaston Park. The balcony tram on its way to Alvaston has just passed council workmen repairing granite sets in the vicinity of the tram stop sign. This was not today's Osmaston Park but rather the one where the Ascot Drive industrial estate is now sited.

Charles McCann did not miss an opportunity for advertising when he sponsored this decorated car float No.51 named 'McCann's Dreadnought' for the Derby Lifeboat demonstration parade on 17 July 1909. The Derby Branch of the Lifeboat Association was formed to raise funds to maintain the lifeboat service.

No effort was spared by Francis Ley to make employment in the service of his firm a pleasure. A magnificent recreation ground adjoined the works for the purpose of cricket, baseball and football. Ley's Vulcan Malleable Iron Foundries were established on Osmaston Road in 1873. The Ley's Cricket Club of 1913, pictured here, had a celebrity on the extreme right of the back row, none other than the versatile sportsman Steve Bloomer prior to his ill-fated coaching trip to Germany.

All sizes and ages of people are fascinated by the solitary private of the Sherwood Foresters guarding the 77mm German field gun captured at Loos by the 15th Division on 25 September 1915. Behind the crowd are the following premises: Old Neptune public house; Hoare & Son, the photographers; Mary Fords tobacconist's; and Ann Roberts newsagent's.

The Farmers' Club at the Derby Agricultural Show appears to have been erected by E.G.Walton & Co.

C.A.Peters Ltd were established in 1885 and were represented at Derby's 1906 Royal Show on stand No.166 as 'merchants and manufactures of Carbotron and Carbolineum'. The company were based in the Derwent Buildings on the Tenant Street corner of the Market Place next to the Royal Oak public house.

J.S.Simnett, the Burton upon Trent photographer, produced a series of views for Derby's 1906 Royal Show and this shows the artistic detail of the grand entrance, a prefabricated timber pavilion specially erected for the show. The site is the park belonging to Osmaston Hall.

A fashion parade of leading Derby gents enjoying a day out at the 1906 Royal Show. The man third from the right was a Mr Thompson.

The Melton Motors Ltd Singer Car Rally entry No.153 was a superb car, registration NU 3018. It was photographed by W.W.Winter, possibly in Markeaton Park during the early 1930s.

A mock boxing match was the theme for this group's contribution to the 1939 Hospital Day Parade through Derby. The 'boxing ring' was constructed on the rear of a flat lorry belonging to Mansfield & Dawson, haulage contractors of 107 Grange Street. Such parades ceased after the DRI and City Hospital were taken in by the NHS on 5 July 1948.

A donkey Barouche was one of the exhibitors at the Derby Show in 1921. The marquees were supplied by Edward Wood & Sons, builders of 70 Park Street, Derby.

The Mikado was the theme for the Mayor of Derby's 1908 carnival.

'Charlie Snort' and 'Sid Hawker' were the main characters on the 'Trent Band Wagon' for this elaborately decorated float for the Hospital Day in 1939. "What abaht your coppers chums?" was the catchphrase for fund-raising for this parade.

'Happiness', 'Loyalty' and 'Super Health' are the messages on the girls' sashes of these members of Derby's Women's League of Health and Beauty parading in the back of an old LMS railway cart. To the right is the events PA system supplied by Willadays Ltd, the electrical and radio engineers of 178 Osmaston Road where vehicle RC 257 advertises their radio's Marconiphone amplifiers. The occasion was probably a fund-raising event for the DRI just after World War Two.

A miniature landau, another exhibit at the 1921 Derby Show.

Another picture in the series depicts a young pony pulling a sedan chair on wheels. The veterinary paddock is in view to the rear right of the marquee.

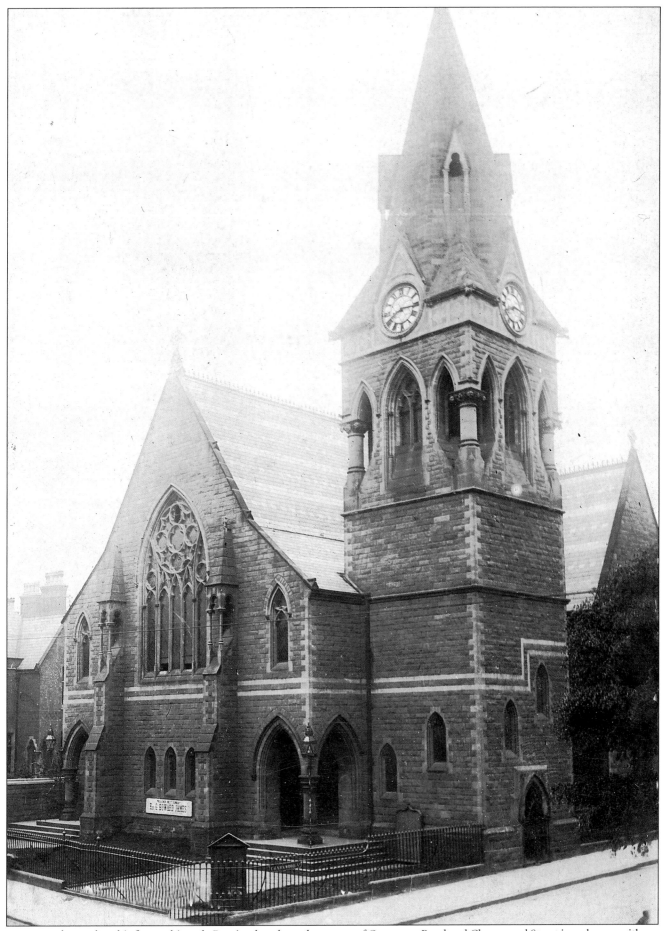

It seems a shame that this fine gothic style Baptist church on the corner of Osmaston Road and Charnwood Street is no longer with us. This General Baptist Chapel was erected in 1861-62 with seating for 900. C.W.Lee is credited with this *c.*1906 view. Since 1971, the site has been occupied by a modern replacement when the old church became dangerous.

The Osmaston Road Baptist Chapel consisted of a chancel, nave, transepts and a tower with a spire. The chancel had stained-glass windows and the baptistery was fitted and lined with marble. This c.1912 interior view was sold at William Tunnicliff's newsagents shop at 101 Osmaston Road. Three stained-glass windows were in memory of the members of this church who fell in World War One.

Bottom left: Edward Bradbury resided at 93 Osmaston Road and was a famous Derby author whose pen name was 'Strephon'. His works included *All About Derbyshire, Pictures of the Peak, Derby China Old & New, Iliffe's Way about Derbyshire,* etc. He was also a major contributor to many magazines and newspapers including the *Illustrated London News, Magazine of Art, Cassell's Magazine, Derbyshire Times, Sheffield Telegraph* etc. Edward also spent 18 years with the Midland Railway at Derby where he was for seven years the chief clerk to J.Sterland Gratton until 1888. This cabinet portrait was taken on 1 May 1879.

Bottom right: Edward's wife was very supportive during his busy life of writing and reviewing. Ada Augusta Bradbury was born in 1860 and died in 1906.

The grand new premises of the Salvation Army on Osmaston Road were constructed during 1907, one year prior to this view. The Salvation Army Citadel was at this time advertising the Young People's Anniversary Celebrations. The adjacent confectionery shop advertising Cadbury's Chocolate belonged to Miss Alice Wilshere.

The 38-strong Derby II Corps' Silver Band are assembled on the steps outside the Salvation Army's Osmaston Road Central Headquarters. The commemorative stones at the rear of the band clearly record the involvement of Alfred Seale Haslam and Mayor Alderman Chambers, and Mrs Holbridge in the stone-laying ceremony of 20 July 1907.

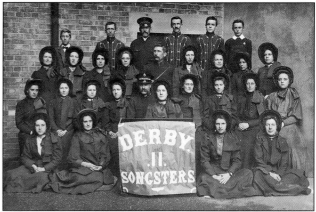

Twenty-one ladies, five men and three boys comprised the Derby II corps of songsters for Derby's Central Salvation Army Choir.

Fourteen charming young Derby Salvation Army girls photographed by F.M.Treble, the Derby photographer, in the 1920s.

A nice portrait of a Derby II Corps band member by Frederick Joseph Boyes of Osmaston Road, c.1911.

A portrait of the bearded William Booth, the Salvation Army's founder, hangs on the right-hand wall where the 48-strong Derby II Corps Band are about to perform in 1929.

The 24 members of the Derby II brass band under the leadership of bandmaster Mr Mathews are pictured here on a real photographic postcard issued in 1912 and sent from 18 Becher Street, Derby.

Twenty-five members of the Derby Central Corps of the Salvation Army were photographed by W.W.Winter during the early 1940s. Note the young triangle player on the front left.

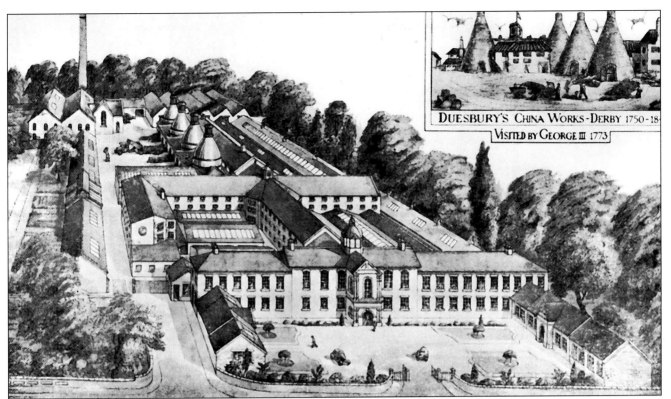

"Crown Derby China is a household word for loveliness the world over." So said the United States' ambassador to Great Britain at Derby on 11 October 1944. The inset (top right) shows Duesbury's China Works in Derby 1750-1848, while the main picture shows the Royal Porcelain Works.

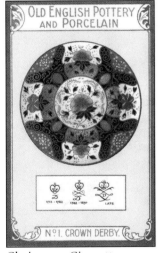

Chairman Cigarettes produced a series of postcards and cigarette cards entitled *Old English Pottery and Porcelain* and this example was No.1 in the series . The Crown Derby marks for 1773-82 and 1782-1850 etc., are shown.

No.23 in the above series shows a double-handed vase which was one of the finest examples of Derby porcelain in the British Museum collection. Marks consisting of an anchor, combined with the letter D, belong to the Derby-Chelsea period made in 1785 in the year before Duesbury's death. The royal blue stripes, rich gilding and delicate flesh tints of the masks together with a classically graceful form make a happy combination rarely surpassed in English porcelain.

No.6 in the series shows the beautiful cup, cover and saucer from the South Kensington Museum. It is noticeable for being fluted and bears the Duesbury Derby mark. It was made in the time of William Duesbury the younger (1786-1811).

Francis William Scarratt, in Derby Market Hall, photographed and published this scarce view, No.1359 in his series, of Derby China titled *The Thistle Dish* by William Pegg the Quaker in 1928.

No.1360 in F.W.Scarratt's 1928 series shows Derby China *Prentice Plate* by William Billingsley, produced in 1796.

No.1358 in F.W. Scarratt's series shows a fine Derby China jug by William Billingsley.

Derby China *The Dancers No.16* was part of F.W. Scarratt's series No.1356 produced again in 1928.

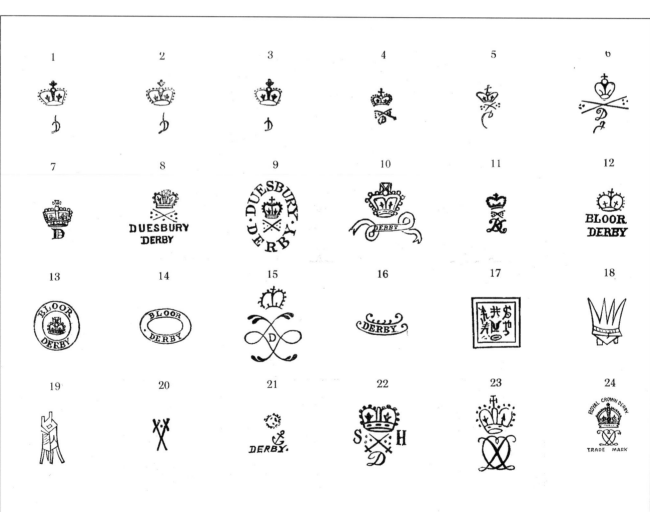

Two Centuries of Progress 1750-1950 is the title of this illustrated guide to Derby China marks. The earliest-known Derby marks were generally in blue.

This photographic postcard was sent to Miss May Smith in the Women's Hospital, Bridge Street, Derby, in November 1908, from 'Bert' at 8 Clarence Road and reads: 'Dear May, This is one of the best results of last night's work. How do you like it? The skating rink at Reginald Street opened about a week ago. In all probability I shall go tonight just to see what sort of a floor they have put down this time. I suppose it is much better this year. Wish you were able to go. I will let you know tomorrow how I get on; L & K, Bert'. The opening sentence leads one to think that Bert was the photographer who captured the bunting and decorations around the roller skating rink on its re-opening night. The reference to the quality of the floor would relate to the fact that the Reginald Street rink was in fact the Corporation Swimming Baths (including Turkish Baths) which was covered over in the winter in order to facilitate roller skating. Reginald Street had been open since April 1904.

This comic view was available in Derby during the Edwardian period in order to advertise the roller skating facilities at Reginald Street Baths and was titled *Picking up a girl at the Derby Skating Rink*. The author can remember going here in the late 1950s to roller skate when the catchphrase 'Follow Flogger' seemed to be in constant use as several people joined at the waist would snake around the rink.

They were known as the New Corporation Baths when they first opened on Reginald Street in 1904. They included Turkish Baths, and Sunray Baths and the first superintendent here was John Mainprize. Constructed in 1903 to designs by John Ward, the Derby Borough surveyor, the opening ceremony was performed by the Mayor Cornelius Boam using a golden key.

Beechwood was the name given to this grand gable and bay-windowed residence complete with stylish gazebo and greenhouse on Osmaston Road. This was Ernest Jorden's residence. In 1904 he ran the Cafe Royal restaurant in Midland Road next door to Winter's the photographers.

W.W. Winter were responsible for this late Victorian cabinet photograph of Frederick Bentley, professor of music, organist etc., who resided at Derwent Villas, Osmaston Road.

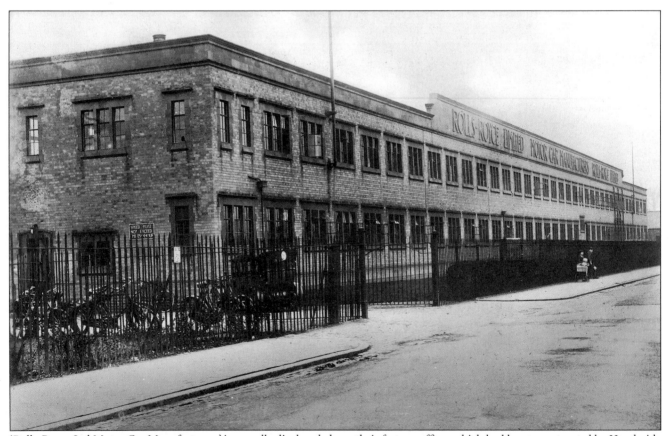

'Rolls-Royce Ltd Motor Car Manufacturers' is proudly displayed above their factory offices which had been constructed by Handyside & Co on an 11-acre site and opened on 9 July 1908. Several workers' cycles are parked inside the gates to the home of the famous Silver Ghost. The gateway on Nightingale Road is now known as No.2 gate.

A view of a specially-adapted vehicle R540 and the Rolls-Royce chauffeurs resting while on a training exercise. The modification was necessary so that several trainee chauffeurs could listen at the same time to the instructions on each journey. The Chauffeurs' School was originally started in the days 'when every motorist of good standing and sensible business men employed a driver whether he himself occasionally took the wheel or not'. The Rolls-Royce factory opened in July 1908 and George Lilley, the Normanton Road photographer, produced this in c.1909.

Most of Derby's larger firms promoted their own sports teams. Rolls-Royce was no exception and this is their Milling No.1 FC team of 1919.

Left: Several Rolls-Royce managers proudly stand with their 1930s football team who have won the Rolls-Royce Association Cup.

Below: John Knifton Ford was a builder just after the turn of the century and he lived in Chellaston House, Chellaston. Richard Weston was also a builder and contractor at this time on Leacroft Road, near Malcolm Street. By 1912 it was Richard Weston & Son while J.K.Ford also had acquired premises at 512 Osmaston Road. This post-war view shows that the union has been completed to form J.K.Ford & Weston Ltd, Derby. The bowler-hatted foreman and his 15 workers are on a building site in Melbourne where local photographer Walter Meynell took this photograph. Messrs Ford & Weston are thought to be those seated on the immediate right. This firm eventually acquired the site on Osmaston Park Road where the Royal Shows were held.

The Derby Co-operative Society Ltd's Peak Bakery appears very neat and uniformly laid out in this *c.*1960s aerial view. The business was off Osmaston Park Road and all the buildings seen in this view belong to the Co-op. The DCS Bakery produced high-class bread and confectionery for over 100,000 members, and their goods were sold everywhere in an area of 400 square miles of here. The site is now Peak Park and houses a large Co-op supermarket.

Uttoxeter Road

The hatted Edwardian children on the left pose for the photographer with their bike and wicker work pram in this mid-1908 view of Uttoxeter New Road looking up towards the Rowditch. The children on the right are at the corner of Junction Street.

The young boy in his overcoat on the left, together with the man with the large basket over his head, are standing on the corner of Junction Street with the corn factors' shop of Mart & Son behind them. To the right lies Parcel Terrace and Thomas Atkin's general store. This view looking up towards the Rowditch was taken in 1908.

This view looking up Junction Street towards Uttoxeter New Road was taken by John Mayle & Sons of 124 Parliament Street in *c.*1895. The occasion was the Junction Street Baptist Sabbath School parade where the Junction Street and surrounding inhabitants wearing their Sunday best have turned out in force. 'Remember Thy Creator in the days of Thy Youth,' and 'Resist Temptation,' is displayed on their banners. The Baptist Sunday School was founded in 1856 and the Baptist Chapel stands on the left. The parade comprises banner bearers, horse and cart, lifeboat float and bandsmen. The chapel has now been demolished and replaced by modern houses.

Fourteen girls and three boys comprised the Junction Street Sunday School junior choir pictured outside the Baptist Chapel in 1912 with the head and two other teachers. They proudly pose with their Sunday School Union framed certificates of merit and other prizes including a metronome.

The well-groomed horse waits for an amateur photographer to take this view of the Junction Street Sunday School juniors ready to start off on their outing in 1922. The horse and cart is parked outside the beerhouse run for several years by Walter Lester, before it eventually became the Junction Tavern. At one time Zachary Smith's brewery of Shardlow owned these premises and latterly Marston's Brewery. Adjacent to this outlet was the well-established Miss E.Hudson's fish dealer's shop.

Twenty-seven girls and 23 boys together with master and mistress comprise this early view of the Junction Street Sunday School Group 15 taken by the photographer of schools and colleges, Bostock & Carr.

This is the continuation of the Junction Street Sunday School Baptist parade seen previously on Junction Street and now on Uttoxeter Old Road. Out of the hundred or so people in view, every single one, adults and children alike, are wearing hats. John Mayle of Parliament Street again took this view in *c.*1895.

A busy Sunday street scene in 1908 has been captured by photographer C.W.Lee with this view looking down Drewry Lane towards Monk Street. On the left stands Thomas Denstone's grocery business. Miss Ellen Weate's corner shop stands at 1 Jackson Street, and was, within a few years, run by Misses Mary and Florence Walker.

Several loaves of bread are just visible on the floor of the ornate cart (under the seat). Joseph John Antliff commissioned this view of himself and his delivery vehicle in 1912 when his bakery and grocery business was situated at 126 Drewry Lane in the former old established grocer's of Thomas Denstone pictured on the previous page. In the 1880s, J.Antliff had a confectionery business in Dean Street and by 1904 he was operating a baker's business from 2 Walter Street.

Below: The severity of the snow storm is evident in this January 1940 view of Jackson Street looking towards the archway and Denstone's grocery shop off Drewry Lane. Locals remember how quickly the snow came and how long it took to disappear in this, the worst winter of World War Two.

C.W.Lee of Pear Tree Studios is credited with taking this view in 1908 looking down Franchise Street towards Peet Street. Many locals are aware of his presence and take up their stance. In the distant right is the junction with Freehold Street where William Henry Williamson had his renowned bakery shop. The Freehold Tavern was on the opposite corner where William Bird was the proprietor at this time.

Yet another 1908 view from C.W.Lee, this time looking up Lynton Street towards Peet Street. The corrugated iron frontage of the Dunkirk Wesleyan Chapel stands on the left. The author can remember going to the youth club here in 1961. Several enamel signs adorn the adjacent shop of George William Gray, while the shops of Miss Betsy Hawley and butcher Charles Morle on either corner of Jackson Street are visible on the middle right. The tall chimney in the distance belongs to J.Bonas & Sons, tape manufacturing mill.

Left: Obviously they were not about to play cricket on this fine day in August 1919, just exactly one month after Derby's Peace Celebrations after World War One. The 36 well-dressed men complete with their club badges were all part of the Roebuck public house cricket club. The Roebuck, a late-Victorian pub, is situated on the Amy Street corner with Stockbrook Street and the long-serving landlord John Walker is believed to be in the centre of the front row with cap in left hand.

Behind Bemrose School the many houses lining Rowditch Avenue and Radcliffe Drive are clearly visible. This late-1930s aerial view shows several peculiar grassy mounds, believed to be air-raid shelters, within the school grounds.

A small group of people are strolling down Uttoxeter Road towards the Rowditch past the clock tower of Bemrose School, opened in 1930, built to the designs of Alexander MacPherson and named after Sir Henry Bemrose (Printer). It took over from the boys' school in Abbey Street.

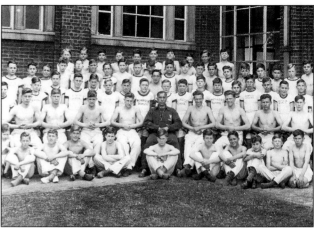

Seventy Bemrose School pupil are pictured in a corner of the school along with their heavily-tanned PE teacher, probably just before World War Two.

The lawn at the rear of the Diocesan Training College is set out for croquet in this view from the north side. 'A Training School for the training of School Mistresses to be employed in educating children of the labouring, manufacturing and other poorer classes' was how the DTC was described in the Trust Deed of 23 February 1850. The founder of the college was Bishop Lonsdale.

P.H.Currey and C.C.Thompson were the architects who produced this artist's impression of the new school building proposed for adding to the New Uttoxeter Road Training College complex in 1908. The new block to the rear housed a fine gymnasium and studio and was built in 1914. A former practising school existed here since 1854, but many revisions and extensions led to the College Primary School which closed in the mid-1990s.

Hurst & Wallis of Sadler Gate produced this south-side view of the Diocesan Training College during 1918. The foundation stone was laid in 1850 and the college was dedicated and opened in 1851 to designs of Mr H.I.Stevens.

The Practising School for Girls and Infants situated within the grounds of the Lichfield Diocesan College for Training School Mistresses stands high in the background. Sixteen young girls under the watchful eye of their teachers are about to dance around the Maypole in this *c*.1907 view by C.W.Lee.

This is Professor A.F.Smith, music and singing master at the Training College during the Edwardian period, whose home was in Friar Gate. The message on the reverse side sent from one of the pupils at Christmas 1906 reads: 'It is bitterly cold here, all the hot water pipes here have gone wrong, I can scarcely hold the pen. We had no early lesson this morning on account of it, so that was one good point of it!'

This was the new block of the Diocesan Training College taken during the early part of 1920. The style was novel at the time.

Elsie and Cressy are amongst these 67 smartly-dressed young ladies at the Diocesan Training College pictured in 1908. 'Elsie' has penned a message to this picture complaining of how hard she is having to work at the college.

The Derby Union Workhouse was the last building on the west side of Uttoxeter Road adjacent to the Derby Borough Asylum. Note the large brass bell push on the left gate pillar where Mrs C.M.Bushell, the matron, is standing in this austere 1908 view by Francis Scarratt. George J.Bushell was the master during this period. The building was completed in four blocks including vagrant and receiving wards, infirmary, schools and a farm attachment. It later became a geriatric hospital ('the Manor') in the 1930s and was demolished in 1990. The Mallard pub and some retail outlets are now on the site.

An insight into the spartan workhouse interior is afforded by this 1908 view of the kitchen with its 47 plates in a huge pine rack. This was under the control of the assistant master, W.Loxham Esq. Even the tall lady on the right would have had a problem in winding the clock or using the high shelf.

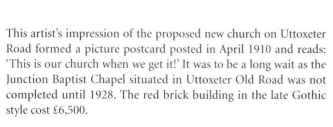

This artist's impression of the proposed new church on Uttoxeter Road formed a picture postcard posted in April 1910 and reads: 'This is our church when we get it!' It was to be a long wait as the Junction Baptist Chapel situated in Uttoxeter Old Road was not completed until 1928. The red brick building in the late Gothic style cost £6,500.

The sheer expanse of the Derby Borough Asylum is captured in this 1906 view taken by C.W.Lee. The asylum stood on Uttoxeter Road, on the Rowditch estate, known as Rough Heanor. The buildings were 280ft above sea level and had a south frontage of nearly 500ft. It accommodated 150 patients of each sex. The grounds covered 27 acres, donated by the Strutt family. The asylum opened in 1888.

Victorian decorative urns flank the driveway up to the grand villa of Albany House in this 1906 view. Private female patients were received into this house situated in its own grounds within the Corporation Estate at Rowditch, Kingsway. The charges here in 1935 varied between two and three guineas per week.

The neatly laid-out forecourt complete with gas lit standard lamp leads to the symmetrically designed hospital of the Borough Asylum.

Not far from the hospital stands the ivy-clad large doctor's house where Samuel Rutherford MacPhail MD, CM, the medical superintendent, resided during the Edwardian period.

Doctors and nursing staff inside the Derby Borough Asylum during January 1907. A Mr Charlie Pratt is one of the pictured nursing staff and the medical superintendent was Dr S.Rutherford MacPhail. The room is heavily adorned with floral arrangements, possibly part of the Christmas arrangements. In 1906 the publication *All about Derby and Neighbourhood* stated: 'It is in all respects a thoroughly up-to-date institution, and one which in appearance, working, and success does credit to the Corporation and the administration.'

Harry J.Cooper was the clerk of the asylum for many years and here he has signed a 1907 decorative maintenance receipt for 11 guineas.

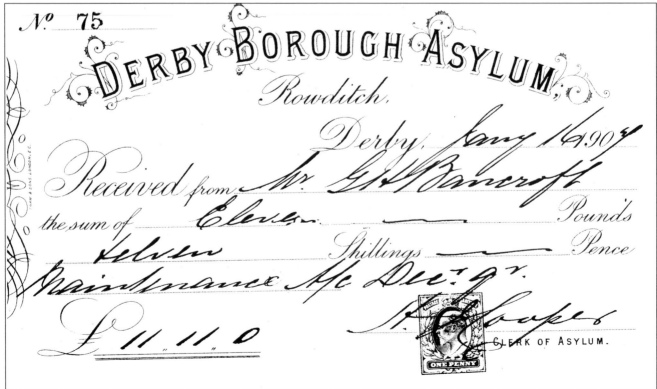

This *c.*1910 view of Kingsway was taken 23 years before the completion of the Town Planning Road No.1 (Kingsway, Queensway and Broadway) in July 1933. All of these neat rockery gardens and fountain were swept away by Derby's Arterial Road (Ring Road). Six Edwardian boys watch William W.Barron & Son, the Borrowash landscape gardeners and nurserymen, at work. The message on the reverse side reads: 'This is a bit of Kingsway but our house is just out of view, it does look nice now it is finished.' Kingsway joined California to New Zealand!

Derby Town Council adopted the scheme for electric tramways in the town on 23 June 1903, letting the contract to J.G.White & Co Ltd of London. Derby Corporation obtained the necessary powers to conduct and operate tramways and to carry out the necessary street widening via the Derby Corporation Act of 1901. The Ashbourne Road and Uttoxeter New Road route opened on 28 November 1907. This comic card was specially produced to commemorate the occasion. The upper destination board 'To Asylums' was particularly pertinent as both the County and the Borough Asylums were on the upper regions of Uttoxeter Road.

Alfred William Woodmansee, the Bold Lane photographer, took this mid-1930s view along the A516 Uttoxeter Road between Cordon Avenue and King's Drive. The extensive building blocks of the new City Hospital, opened on 11 November 1929, dominate the background. Built on the pavilion style to designs by T.H.Thorpe, work began on this site in 1926. The Town Council took it over on 1 April 1931 and it was recognised as one of the most up-to-date in the country.

Bits & Pieces

In the centre of the pack, sitting behind the decorated umbrella, is C.Bowins the Brown Owl of her 21st Brownie Pack. The Derby Girl Guides' Association HQ was at 116 Osmaston Road.

Frederick Boyes, the Derby photographer, took this individual photograph of C.Bowins.

These spartan surroundings were the quarters of the 3rd Derby Company of the Girl Guides. 'God first, others next, self last,' was their motto. Portraits of Lord and Lady Baden Powell hang either side of the fireplace.

A very happy group of 15 Derby boys with only one pair of long trousers between them. Probably a local boys' club in Markeaton Park.

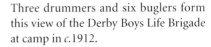

An amateur photographer has recorded the successful 1st Derby Boys Brigade Football Club during the 1912-13 season.

Three drummers and six buglers form this view of the Derby Boys Life Brigade at camp in c.1912.

Another view at the same camp, *c.*1912, shows 20 or so boys forming the orderly department of the Derby Boys Life Brigade. It is obviously pot-washing time.

A.E.Maskrey has stepped forward to collect his third prize medal for the 100 yards sprint from Miss Johnson, daughter of then Mayor of Derby, Samuel Johnson, on 10 June 1914 at the newly-opened municipal training ground on Markeaton Recreation grounds, with its large circular grass track.

The Diana Studios of St Peter's Street produced this scarce picture of the first Derby Shop Anti-Vivisection campaign. The group had 400 members and between 21 March to 29 March 1934 they collected 2,785 signatures. The honorary secretary Mr H.M.Nesbitt Wood, complete with bow tie, and campaign petition helpers are seen in the doorway of the former Derbyshire Building Society's office on the corner of Victoria Street and Green Lane after it was empty following their move to Irongate.

There are only five boys out of 30 pupils in this group who are showing off their prize and trophy from a music competition when this Derby school competed with other local schools. Does anyone know what 'Cennick' stood for?

During 1911, Harry Bishtons Foster brought his unique tractor 'John Bull' No.3444, complete with loads, to Derby.

Charles William Lee produced this interesting scene from his Pear Tree Studio during 1907. Over 100 ladies, young and old, are gathered here in their finery. The occasion is unknown but may have been Women's Suffrage.

The printing firm of Knight Bros & Cooper Ltd of Devonshire Street published this c.1912 photograph showing the enchanting Doreen M.Elliott. But who was she?

Baby is asleep in her wooden and wicker pram in this delightful scene set around a hay wagon and titled *A Derby Party, 1907*.

The last picture in the book must belong to C.W.Lee our back street photographer. He has recorded the corner of Porter Road and Almond Street in 1908. Several Edwardians are gathered close to Morton's habadashery shop. This is one of many photographs to appear in a future publication of the Normanton area.

The Derby Alphabet

To close this book on Derby, its roads, back streets and landmarks, the following *Derby Alphabet,* believed to date from the late 1840's, is a fitting song with which to end.

Now come listen unto me, while we are met,
And I'll relate to you the Derby Alphabet:

A   for Arboretum, a lovely place to see

B   stands for Bloom Street, they're always on the spree

C   stands for Curzon Street, with the Temperance Hall so grand where Uncle Ned says "Go ahead" with the Allelulia Band

D   stands for Darley Grove, where all the pretty girls go arm in arm o' summer nights, a walking with their swells

E   stands for Eagle Street where they often dance and sing

F   stands for Friar Gate, where Townley he did swing

G   for the Grapes in Green Lane, Mr Doris's abode

H   stands for High Street, somewhere up London Road.

I   is for the Irongate, where I weekly give a call

J   for Jerry the pieman, known to all

K   stands for King Street, there's lots of preaching done,

L   stands for London Road, where Birkham he did run

M   for the Midland Railway — the pleasant looks the porters give

N   is for the Neptune, where Charlie William lived

O   is for Osmaston Park, with its daisies white and red

P   stands for Park Street, you'll find the Lantern's Head

Q   stands for Queen Street, you'll find it if you search. Rum and gin at the Tiger Inn, opposite St Michael's Church

R   is for the Racecourse, a handsome little stand, Admired by all the lords and ladies in the land

S   is for Siddals Lane, where employment none can get, Turner's Mill is standing still and plenty more to let

T   is for Tommy Godderidge, who in Derby may be found

U   is for the union, take my advice and save you blunt, And keep out of the big house there with the ivy in the front

V   is for Victoria Street, the widest in the town

W   for Walker Lane, a place of great renown

X   double X for sparkling ales, and sparkling wines so clear

Y   is for Yeoman Cavalry that assembles once a year

Z   And now as I lie here cosy in my bed I will try to think of something that begins with letter Z